CAPTAIN BENJAMIN CHURCH
—and the—
KING PHILIP'S WAR

AS TOLD BY JOSHUA TEMPLE

JAMES DUNN

Copyright © 2021 by James Dunn

ISBN   Softcover   978-1-953537-91-1

All rights reserved. No part of this book may be reproduced or transmitted in any form or by any means, electronic or mechanical, including photocopying, recording, or by any information storage and retrieval system without express written permission from the author, except in the case of brief quotations embodied in critical reviews and certain other non-commercial uses permitted by copyright law.

Printed in the United States of America.

To order additional copies of this book, contact:
Bookwhip
1-855-339-3589
www.bookwhip.com

CONTENTS

List of Names v

Chapter 1   Valley Forge Pennsylvania 1778 and
            the tale of the Great Swamp Fight 1

Chapter 2   The Death of Sassamon 11

Chapter 3   The War begins 20

Chapter 4   Bloody Creek 48

Chapter 5   The Captivity of Mary Rowlandson 54

Chapter 6   The Hero Leaves 64

Chapter 7   The War Drags On 76

Chapter 8   The Town of Sudbury 82

Chapter 9   Captain Benjamin is Back 93

Chapter 10 The Hunt is On 104

Chapter 11 Annawon 118

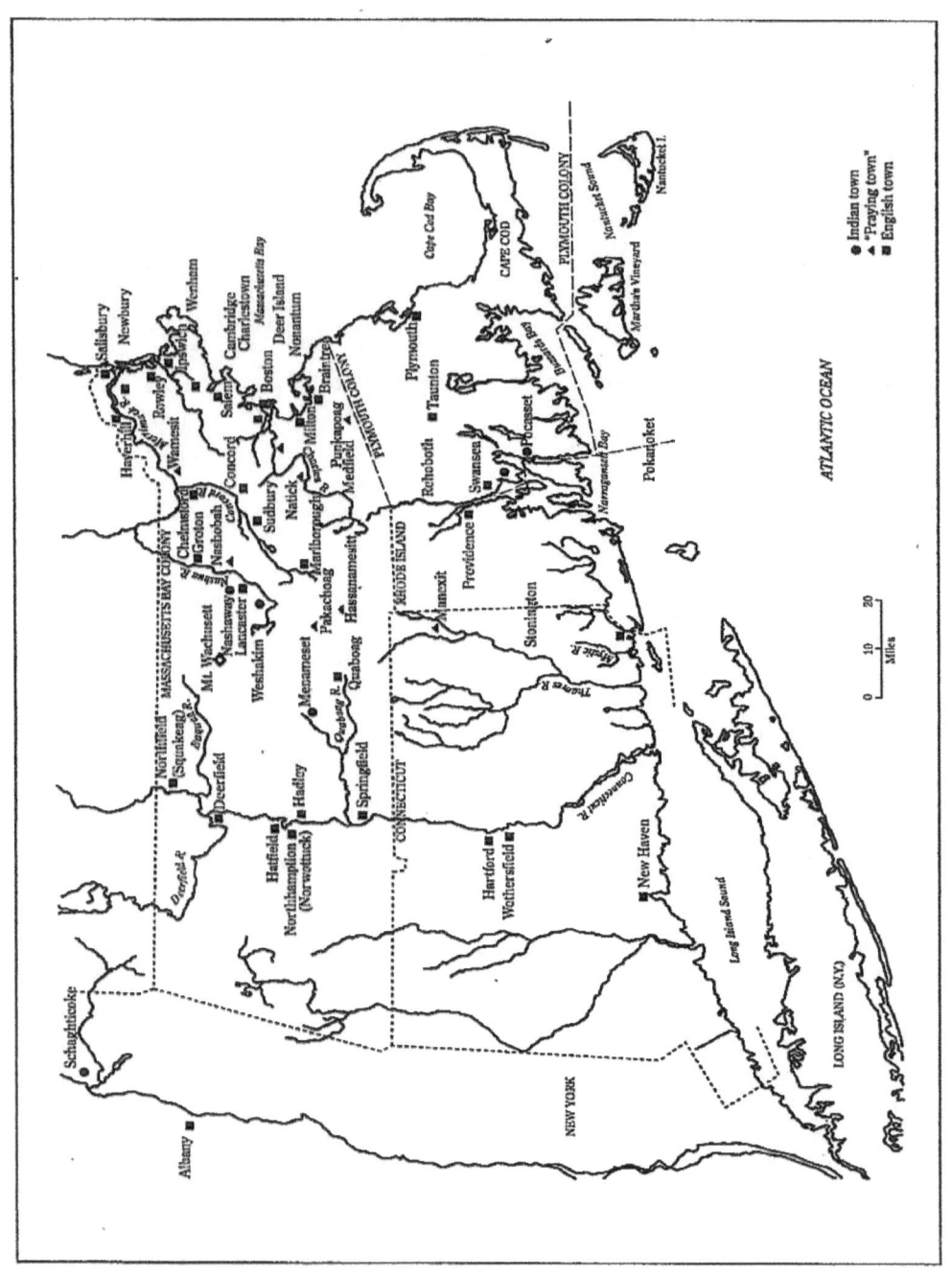

Map of New England circa 1675

Sourcemap: Handbook of North Americans (gen. ed., William C. Stuartevant), vol. 15: Northeast, ed. Bruce G. Trigger (Washington Smithsonian Institution, 1978), p.161.

LIST OF NAMES

A

Agawam - Indian tribe of the Springfield Massachusetts area.

Annawon - Chief Counsellor of Philip's and last Indian warrior chief captured in the war.

Andros, Edmund - English Governor of New York.

Appleton, Captain Samuel - of Ipswich became the Commander of the Western theatre (the Connecticut River Valley) replacing Pynchon.

Assawompsett Pond in modern Lakeville.

Awashonks - female sachem of the Sakonnets

Ayes, Sergeant John - Citizen of Brookfield Massachusetts who was killed while on a peace mission to the Nipmuck tribe. His garrison house was also the center of the battle in Brookfield.

B

Brattle, Thomas was one of the three emissaries sent from Massachusetts to speak peace terms to the Wampanoags, which failed miserably on June 25th 1675.

Beers, Captain Richard - A Captain of the Massachusetts Colony from Watertown died outside of Squakeag.

Barrow, Sam - The English name of Sanballat, father of Totoson and an attacker of the Clark Garrison.

Bradford, Major William - a Major in charge of the Plymouth Colony army.

Brocklebank, Captain Samuel - The leader of the Massachusetts troops stationed at the Marlborough supply depot. He and many of his men were killed at the Sudbury fight.

Bull, Jireh - A trader and owner of the garrison at Pettaquamscut deep in Narragansett country where the United Colonies gathered for the Great Swamp Fight.

C

Canonchet - A Narragansett Sachem who led the attack on Providence.

Careswell - Is the name of the Winslow manner in Marshfield.

Church, Alice - wife to Benjamin church, first son Thomas, they lived in Duxbury, fled to Portsmouth on Aquidneck Island during the war, then settled in Little Compton.

Church, Benjamin - grandson of Richard Warren, a Mayflower passenger.

Conway, Peter - Praying Indian who spied on the Nipmucks and helped to release Mary Rowlandson from captivity.

Cudworth, Captain James - was the Plymouth Army commander in June

Curtis, Ephraim - A merchant and trader with the Indians in the Brookfield area. A fighter at Marlborough also.

D

Dublet, Tom (Indian name Nepanet) - Praying Indian who spied on the Nipmucks and helped to secure the release of Mary Rowlandson from captivity.

Deer Island - A small Island in the Boston harbor where Indians were transported to where many died of exposure or lack of food.

E

Elliot - Minister to the Indians. He printed the first Indian Bible, of which no copies still exist.

F

G

George, Honest - A Sakonnet Indian who was the go-between for Benjamin Church and Awashonks.

Goulding, Captain Roger - The captain who rescued Church and company from the Pease Field fight.

Gookin

H

Henchman, Captain Daniel - chosen army Commander of 100 men by Massachusetts Colony.

Hutchinson, Captain Edward (son of Ann Hutchinson) head of the Massachusetts emissary group sent to the Narragansetts to assure peace. Also led the fateful peace negotiations attempt in Brookfield.

Hoar, John - English friend to the Indians and negotiator for Mrs. Rowlandson's release.

Hubbard, William - A seventeenth Century clergyman and historical writer.

I

J

Joslin, Goodwife Ann - A captive along with Mary Rowlandson out of Lancaster who was killed by the Indians.

John, Sagamore - Leader of the Nipmuck tribe who brought his former chief into Boston as a peace offering to the English.

K

L

Lathrop, Captain Thomas - Of Beverley, Massachusetts Colony captain died at Bloody Brook leading refugees from Deerfield.

Leverett, Governor John - The Governor of the Massachusetts Colony.

Lightfoot - A Sakonnet Indian who became a lieutenant in Church's company.

M

Magistrates - Plymouth ruling body.

Mather, Reverend Cotton - Boston preacher and historical writer.

Mattashunnamo/Mattachunnamo - alleged murderer of Sassamon.

Matoonas Nipmuck sachem responsible for the attack on Mendon. He was turned into Boston by his own men at the end of the war.

Massasoit, Sachem, chief of the Wampanoag Indians at the time of the landing of the Puritans in the Mayflower.

Moseley, Captain Samuel - A sea captain who became a captain in the Massachusetts Colony Army. His band was a ruthless band of former pirates who persecuted all Indians including friendly ones.

Mount Hope - The Peninsula on the western end of Plymouth Colony that just out into Mount Hope Bay and the top of the Narragansett River. It was the home to Philip's Wampanoags. Today it encompasses Bristol and Warren Rhode Island.

N

New Amsterdam - New York city while under Dutch control. It changed its name in 1664 when the colony of New Netherland became the colony of New York, under English control.

Newbury, Captain Benjamin - A Connecticut commander sent to Hadley to bolster the area after the attack on an Indian fishing camp.

Nipmucks - The Indian tribe that lived in central Massachusetts around Wachusett Mountain.

Nompash - Chief warrior of the Sakonnets.

Nunnuit, Peter - (Indian name was Petonwowet) was the son of Sakonnet leader Awashonks and was an emissary to Governor Winslow.

O

James Oliver one of three emissaries sent from Massachusetts to speak peace terms to the Wampanoags, which failed miserably on June 25th 1675.

Oneko, A Chief of the Mohegans, his son who led the Mohegans against Philip in Smithfield.

Oliver Cromwell - Puritan leader of England who overthrew the king and became Lord Protector of England.

P

Patuckson - witness in the trail of Sassamon's death.

Pessacus - one of the Narragansett chiefs.

Penacook - The Indian tribe around the Merrimack River who remained neutral during the war.

Peterson, Simon infantryman from Massachusetts who deserted.

Pequots - Indian tribe in eastern Connecticut.

Pequot War - War in 1637 between the Pequot Indians of Connecticut were the Connecticut man allied with the Mohegan Tribe and Massachusetts Colony to put down a threat by the Pequot tribe. The Plymouth Colony was supposed to join as well, but the war was short and over with before they could muster their men.

Philip, Metacom, Sachem, King of the Wampanoag tribes.

Pierce, Captain Michael - A Plymouth captain who was killed along with about 40 men near the Pawtucket River, northeast of Providence.

Phipps, Corporal Solomon - leader of a troop of calvary troops at the Sudbury fight.

Praying Indian - An Indian who had converted to Christianity. Many lived in separate villages between Indian tribe and the English.

Prentice, Captain Thomas - A commander of a mounted troop.

Pocassets - The Indian tribe, part of the Wampanoag tribe that lived on the north eastern side of the Sakonnet River now Tiverton Rhode Island, and Fall River Massachusetts.

Poor, Salem a former slave who paid for his freedom and fought at Breed's Hill (better known as Bunker Hill) in Boston during the American Revolution. Commended by fourteen officers.

Pynchon John, of Springfield, civic leader, merchant, Indian trader, first leader of the Western theatre for the Massachusetts Colony army.

Q

Quinnapin - A Narragansett chief who was the master to Mary Rowlandson.

Quaiapin - female leader of one of the Narragansett tribes.

R

Rowlandson, Reverend Joseph - Preacher in Lancaster Massachusetts whose wife, Mary, had been taken captive.

Rowlandson, Mary - Wife of Reverend Joseph Rowlandson who was taken captive from her Lancaster home by the Nipmuck tribe.

S

Sakonnets - Indian tribe that was part of the larger Wampanoag tribe. Their home was the territory on the south eastern side of the Sakonnet River, now Little Compton Rhode Island.

Sanford, Major - The owner of the Portsmouth Rhode Island home that Benjamin Church and his wife lived in during the war.

Savage, Captain Thomas was one of three emissaries sent from the Massachusetts Colony to speak peace terms to the Wampanoags, which failed miserably on June 25th 1675.

Sassamon, John - Interpreter to Philip as well as a relative by marriage. He was the son-in-law to Philip's sister, Amie.

Southworth, Constant Plymouth Colony war treasurer, magistrate and father-in-law to Benjamin Church.

Smith, Corporal Ebenezer, infantryman from Vermont.

T

Talcott, Major John - Commander of Connecticut Army men from Hartford.

Tefft, Joshua - Turn - coat Englishman who join the Indian cause.

Temple, Bridget - Wife to Joshua Temple and cook for their hut.

Temple, Joshua - Story teller of Captain Benjamin Church and the King Philips War.

Tispaquin - A Wampanoag chief who was also known as the "Black Sachem."

Treat, Major Robert - Commander of Connecticut army troops on the Connecticut River.

Tobias - One of Sassamon's alleged murderers and a counselor to Philip. He was the father to Wampapaquan.

Tispaquin, the Black Sachem, brother-in-law to Philip and one of his counselors

Totoson - sachem from of the Mattapoisett tribe Buzzards Bay. He led the attack on the Clark House Garrison in Plymouth.

Turner, Captain William - Connecticut captain in Hadley Massachusetts who led a rag-tag group of civilians, 160 strong to a fishing camp of Indians on the Connecticut River. He was killed there.

U

The United Colonies - an association of the three Colonies of Connecticut, Plymouth, and Massachusetts formed during the Pequot War in 1637. It was formed as a protective force in case of Indian attacks. An attack on one was an attack on all. Rhode Island was excluded from the association.

Uncas - Chief of the Mohegans.

V

W

Wadsworth, Captain Samuel - A Massachusetts captain who led 70 men to the fight at Sudbury where he and many of his men died.

Wannalancet - the chief of the Penacook who stayed out of the war by going north.

Wootonekanusk - Philip's wife who was captured late in the war.

Wequogan, the chief of the Agawam Indians of Springfield Massachusetts.

Weetamoo - The female leader of the Pocassets.

Willard, Major Simon the Connecticut Colony army military leader who saved Brookfield in its second day of attack by the Nipmucks.

Williams, Roger - Founder of Rhode Island who was chased out of the Massachusetts Colony over doctrinal differences. He befriended the Narragansett Indians and founded Providence RI. He was able to get a charter from the King of England for a new, if small colony. It would take many years but in 1663, Williams finally had his charter for Rhode Island and the Providence Plantations.

Wampapaquan - son of Tobias, alleged witness to Sassamon's death

Josiah Winslow - Governor of Plymouth in 1675. Presided over Sassamon's murder case. There were 12 English jurors and six Praying Indians who found three Indians guilty of Sassamon's' death.

Weetamoo - female sachem of the Pocassets, (from the Tiverton area.)

X

Y

Z

CHAPTER ONE

Valley Forge Pennsylvania 1778 and the tale of the Great Swamp Fight

English attack Narragansett fort in the Great Swamp Attack.
executedtoday.com

It is the end of a long cold day of training for George Washington's troops at Valley Forge. Washington had just recently introduced his men to a new trainer. First, he would train a core of 100, who in turn would train the others. They trained on the open fields of Valley Forge, a former iron forge 20 miles northwest of Philadelphia, the one-time Capital of the new nation, but recently captured by the British. In conventional European standards of warfare, capturing the capital, or major commercial and manufacturing ports and cities determined the victors of the battle. The British were now in control of Boston, New York and Philadelphia, surely the rebels would give up. But General

Washington, and the Colonial government refused to surrender when they should have, they continued to fight, even when they lost, which they did often. So, when the fledgling American government was driven out of the capital, Washington took his 12,000-man army into the hills of Valley Forge overlooking Philadelphia to rest, recuperate and to rebuild. One of the people who had come into the fold at Valley Forge, the new trainer was Baron Friedrich Wilhelm August Heinrich Ferdinand von Steuben. He had been born in Prussia, grew up in Russia, and trained under the greatest general of Europe at the time, Frederick the Great of Prussia. As the leader of tiny Prussia Frederick was able to fight off three major powers, Russia, Austria and France at the same time. (It has been said that Prussia was not a state that contained an army, but an army that contained a state.) Von Steuben had been in the French embassy when Benjamin Franklin was the American Ambassador there. Franklin convinced him to join the French military forces, including Marquis de Lafayette, that were going to aid the Americans. Von Steuben would be the one to teach the American Regulars to fight with the discipline of a European army. The Americans needed to learn how to defeat the British in the field of battle, pitting massive forces against massive forces. That way they could drive the English army out of the American lands. Until then Washington's troops sat outside of Philadelphia. French engineers helped the Americans to build an impenetrable defense system overlooking the Southeastern approaches from Philadelphia. The encampment bordered the Schuylkill River to the North the Valley Creek stream to the west which emptied into the Schuylkill. So even though the defeated American troops where within striking distance of the British, there were reasons why they did not. The Americans were well fortified, they had French help, and most European armies rested during the winter and reengaged the battle when the spring came. Plus, the winter was as frigidly cold as any in the area had ever seen it. The rivers, the supply roads of the 1700's were frozen over. Add to that, the fact that the British could relax and sleep warmly in Philadelphia during the winter; like the Hessians at Trenton had done two years earlier, then send their troops out to crush the rebels in the spring, they had no worries.

So, Washington's and Von Steuben's job were to forge the Americans into a strong fighting force at a place where iron was once produced. When the drilling was done for the day, the men broke up and headed to their barracks, mere log cabin huts windowless 14 foot by 12 foot with a small fire place that housed Washington's 12,000 troops. Their food was cooked in an earthen beehive oven of sorts behind the huts. The cook might have been one of the wives who would have to share her sleeping quarters, not only with her husband, but 10 or 11 other men. Not many women ventured to do so, but the war had made some of these women homeless, their only place was with their men in the huts. There were 400, maybe 500 hearty women who dared to put up with this arrangement. They were the cooks, the seamstress's, the nurses, of this ragtag army that Von Steuben and Washington would forge into a world class fighting force.

"That Von Steuben is a horse's ass," says Corporal Ebenezer Smith as he barges into the log cabin barracks, one of thousands that housed George Washington's Regular army. "He can't even speak English. 'Eins zwei, drei nachlinks, Eins zwei drei nachrechts, eins zwei drei. Halten sie, zielen sie, schiessen. Dummkopf, Ich gesage schiessen!' Is that all we do until spring is march and march and march. Learn how to load a gun, I know how to load a gun. I've been doing it since I was 10. And it is so damn cold here."

"You think it's cold Smithie?" says Joshua Temple. "You should have been in Narragansett during the King Philips War. Those men there, they knew cold," he says as he warms himself by the dying embers of the barracks fire as he prods the embers with his bayonet. "They had to march at the beginning of the coldest winter known to man. Fifty to 60 miles from Plymouth to the Narragansett tribe country as a winter storm was brewing. They arrived in Warwick Rhode Island, next to the water, wind blowing in, but at least they found shelter in John Smith's trading post and the farms around it. But it wasn't their last stop. They were marching to fight the fierce Narragansetts, with winter coming on them. They were going to fight their enemies and the winter."

"Yeah, you and your Indian fighters. I hate you almost as much as I hate Von Steuben," said Smith.

"That's all right, and if you don't learn from Von Steuben you'll end up as dead as those who didn't learn from Captain Benjamin Church," said Temple.

"Your hero, Church," Smith scoffed. "How does he help you get through a day of Von Driller?"

"Benjamin Church taught his men to fight like the Indians did," says Temple. " At first the men didn't want any part of it. They hated the Indian way of fighting. It was cowardly they said, unmanly. They didn't want to fight like the savages, they would say. The problem was that those savages were beating them in battle after battle. It wasn't until the Battle at Narragansett were, we got an advantage. And that was because we came in with 1000 men from all over New England. Men from Plymouth, from Massachusetts, from Connecticut with aid from Rhode Island."

"Plymouth is Massachusetts. You're as dumb as Von Steuben," Smith shouts.

"Shows you what you know. In 1675, when the war started, Plymouth and Massachusetts were separate colonies. The King decided to make them one single colony after the war," replied Temple.

"Yeah, sure," said Smith. "So how cold was it."

"The coldest winter in years, said Temple. "But that wasn't the worst of it. They were supposed to meet-up with a supply ship from Aquidneck Island, but it was blocked from coming to shore by the ice in the water."

"You mean they had no food" said Jacob Anderson, another soldier listening into the conversation. "Things never change do they. Cold and hungry, a soldier's fate."

"That's right, they had very little food. Just what the farmers could give 700 men. That is 700 hungry men, says Temple. They had one night of fairly warm accommodations and then they were marching again, 19 miles with a snowstorm brewing up. They were to march to Jireh Bull's garrison at Pettaquamscut deep in Narragansett country. There they were to meet up with the men marching in from Connecticut, 300

Englishmen, who also brought with them over 100 Mohegan Indians. The Garrison was a stone building, and thought impenetrable. Well after marching the 19 miles they got to where the farm was supposed to be."

"Supposed to be, what did they get lost?" asks Anderson.

"Yeah, they had Von Steuben leading them," says Smith. "'Eins zwei drei Marsch, eins zwei drei, wo aus wir, 'Where are we?'" All the men laugh."

"No, they weren't lost," says Temple, "they were where they were supposed to be. The farm that they were going to rendezvous at had been burned down by the Indians. It was late in the evening, it was dark and cold, and they had to wait for the Connecticut men to get there. They had to sleep out in the open, no tents, on the ground, just like animals. It was freezing cold that night as the snow covered them where they laid. I don't know how you sleep in those conditions. By the time they got up in the morning, frostbite had crippled some. But the Connecticut men joined them and they marched on."

"So, Von Steuben did show up," said Smith, laughter erupts again.

Yeah, right, so you think it is cold here. At least we have this shelter. We are not sleeping out in the field like an animals," says Temple. Temple continues to stir the fire with his bayonet and warms his hands by the low embers. A young boy stands behind the men with an armful of logs for the fire. He had been standing behind the men, listening to them argue until his arms were heavy with the load of wood. One of the men sees him.

"Make way for more firewood," he yells above all the other voices.

The men make a path for the boy, one of the drummer boys, who also bunked in this hut. All the men huddled around to gather in a little bit of the expected warmth as the fire bursts into fresh flames with the fresh fuel.

"So, what happened after they start marching again," asked Tobias (Toby) Cummings, the young boy who had brought the wood.

"Ah, lad you want to hear the story again," Smith says sarcastically.

"Leave him alone," says Temple. "He may not have heard it. Besides where are we going?"

"To march off into the snow," said Smith.

"Yeah, you can go march with Von Steuben," the barracks erupts with laughter again. "I'm going to stay here by the fire and talk about Benjamin Church," says Temple. "Come sit by the fire, Toby. We'll talk the night away."

Toby jumped to a spot close to the fire, and looked eagerly to listen to Joshua Temple as if he were going to listen to his favorite uncle. He sat at his feet to soak in every word and warmed himself by the fire at the same time.

"Ohhhh, it was cold that night. The next day when they marched off, some men couldn't even walk, some fell by the wayside. Your fingers were so cold you didn't even know if you could pull the trigger on you gun, never mind reload it. But they marched on anyhow to the Indian fort. They were guided by a captive Indian who had a falling out with the Narragansetts and now led the Colonists, plus some Mohegans, 1000 strong in all. They marched for hours and got there early in the afternoon. In front of them was the biggest Indian fort that the English had ever seen. It was as tall, or taller than any stockade fence around any fort that the English had built. There were bands of Indians outside of the fort and they fired at the English before they ran into the fort. We went all around the tree and mud walls until we came to an open end."

"Were you there?" Toby asked incredulously.

"No, dear boy," Temple said laughing. "This battle happened a hundred years ago. But there are a lot of lessons for today, like dealing with the weather," he says raising his voice so Smith can hear him.

"You're daft," Smith replies.

Temple smiles, "Where was I, yes we, err, the Englishmen...."

"We're Americans," Toby interrupts proudly.

"Yes, we are, we are Americans, but we used to be Englishmen. We will create something new, something better. A new country, 13 states, united for common defense. Just like the United Colonies in King Philips War. It will have local governments, controlled by the people of the states, elected by the people. No more kings and queens thousands of miles away dictating to us how we should live or do business. Free men ruling themselves. Now hush-up and I'll go on with the story," Temple admonishes the boy.

"Yes sir," Toby replies meekly.

"So, the Englishmen were moving their way carefully around the Indian fort trying to avoid the shots coming down from inside. The Connecticut men had been in the lead of the march and had gotten there first. They found an opening at one end of the fort, it appeared to be an unfinished end. The fort had been built in a swamp, the fort itself being on a portion of dry ground obviously. Normally the water that surrounded the fort would be a sort of natural moat that would slow the Englishmen down, but since it was so cold all the swamp was frozen. There was a fallen tree that bridged the gap that led to the opening of the fort and dropped off to the ice below. This was either a Godsend opening for the Englishmen, or a planned trap to draw the them in as the Indians fired madly at them. The Connecticut men did not wait for the others, who were not far behind. They rushed into the opening and the Indians laid down a merciless round of fire that took out many of the attackers. Soon the men from Massachusetts and Plymouth came to the mouth of the fort adding supporting fire for the Connecticut men and sent more men in. Robert Mosely, a miserable dastardly man who led a group of pirates and near-do-wells…"

"Pirates?" Toby repeats shockingly.

"Yes pirates," Temple says with a wink. "They had been in jail at the outbreak of the war and when the elders decided it was more important to have men, and I use that term loosely, animals would be a better word to describe them, when they decided it was better having them fighting the Indians rather than hanging them, they were given a choice. Fight or hang, obviously, they choose to fight. Moseley had been a former sea-captain and could control them, but then the elders couldn't control Moseley, or they didn't want to."

"Wow," Toby says completely enthralled.

"Yes, anyhow, Moseley's men might have been scoundrels, but they fought well. He and his men follow the Connecticut men into the fort. The English start making headway inside the fort. Our friend Benjamin Church was sitting on his horse with Governor Josiah Winslow, the commander-in-chief of the whole attack and he was getting impatient and wanted to join the battle. He asked Winslow to allow him to take some men and go inside. Winslow tells him to go ahead. Church gathers about 30 willing soldiers and heads inside. He instantly recognizes one of the men, Captain Gerdner, just as he is shot in the head and drops to the ground. Not realizing he had been shot, Church goes to the aid of his friend, only to discover the mortal wound. But he determined that the kill shot had come from behind them, that there where Indians outside of the fort, coming behind the intruders, again making the opening look more like a trap, than a weakness in the fort. Church realizes that he has to take his men outside of the entry and find the enemy shooting in. He and some of his men get outside into the brush. Church saw an Indian who waved for him to come forward. Church hoped he might be a friendly with information. He told his men not to shoot at him, but one of the last men to come out of the fort to help out, shot and killed the Indian. Then they spied a group of Indians and Church gave firing orders to his men to shoot them when they rose to fire at the Englishmen in the opening. As the Indians rose, one of the English guards yelled to Church not to fire upon them because they were Friendly Indians, the Mohegans from Connecticut. The guard was wrong, they were the enemy. After firing they ran into the fort and upon the misinformed guard. But Church and his men were still hidden outside as more Indians approached, 'a black heap of them' as Church described them. There would be no mistaking this time. Again, he encouraged his men again not to fire upon them until they rose up to shoot at the entrance to the fort. They rose up to fire their muskets, and Church's men being behind them, fired a volley, killing many and scattering those who survived. About a dozen ran into the fort and into a "hovel" a shelter near the opening of the fort. Church's men reloaded and ran up to the shelter where the Indians ran and hid, but one of the Narragansetts had a gun pointed at Church. Ignoring the danger to himself, he ordered his men to attack. He was struck with three bullets, one to his abdomen, which only broke his skin, another took out a pair of mittens in his coat pocket, but a third dug into his thigh, grazing his hip bone and giving him a considerable wound. Still, he was able to get a shot off at the man who shot him. One of his men came to his aid and supported him, he was shot with an arrow as Church encouraged his men to continue battling the enclosure. The English were forced to draw back off of this part of the fight, but they were well within the fort. Church could see that some of the English were setting fire to the wigwams inside the fort. He protested and he was told that they were under order of General Winslow to burn it down. He ordered them to hold off until he could talk to the general. So, he headed back outside to find the General."

"As he is being tended to by his aide, he sees Winslow and Church tells him to reverse the order. He had seen stores of food in baskets throughout the fort in the wigwams inside. They could stay in the fort throughout the night, eat the food, wait out the storm that was still raging outside and leave later. Just before Winslow gives the countermanding order Moseley appears, he also had heard the conversation and he threatens Winslow. He tells him that he will shoot his horse out from under him if he countermands the order. Church tries to argue with Moseley as a doctor with Winslow tells Church if he continues to argue to spare the fort, he will not treat Church and he can bleed to death. Whether Church gave into the threat, or was getting weak from losing blood, or seeing that he was outvoted, he quit arguing. The doctor tended to Church, and the fort was set on fire, killing most of the people still stuck inside, and now the Englishmen had to get out, regroup and then march the nineteen miles back to Warwick and to Smith's house. Church's wound was so bad, he had to ride in a cart. Since it was December 19th almost the shortest day of the year, the sun was setting around 4:00 in the afternoon. The men, whole or wounded had to march through the night. Some of the wounded did not last through the march. Church did. They started to arrive at Smith's farm around 2:00 in the morning. Still there was very little food, but at least the men had shelter, whether it was in farmer's houses, or barns they could be fairly warm. The supply ship was able to make it into the shore, off load its supplies and take some of the more badly wounded to Newport on

Aquidneck island. Church went to Newport and stayed there for about a month healing-up."

"Wow," said Toby. "Did Mr. church go back into the fight? How did the war start, how many people died at the Indian fort? Do men always argue in a fight?"

"So many questions," young man. "We'll pick-up the story tomorrow night. Go get some shut-eye now."

"Do I have to?" complains Toby.

"Yes, you do, you don't want to get Von Steuben mad at you for being late to roll call, he'll have you whipped," warns Temple.

"Oh boy, not me. Shut-eye, here I come," Toby yells as he runs to his bunk.

Temple just chuckles.

CHAPTER TWO

The Death of Sassamon

History of Massachusetts.org

The next day was another long one filled with endless, repetitive drilling. Von Steuben and his aides were relentless. It seemed as if Von Steuben enjoyed drilling and insulting the men, in German of course. Then Captain Benjamin Walker, his aide would translate the insults into English for those who couldn't figure out what he was saying. Since the drilling only included part of the command, there would always be an audience of men watching, laughing and mocking anyone who slipped up. Von Steuben played up to those watching, because even that was an opportunity to teach. Finally, as the skies started to darken, the drilling ended and it was time for chow. It looked more like the swill that you would feed the swine. Temple asked, "Who are we, the Prodigal Son?" who looked at swine food wishing he could eat it.

"You'll eat it and be happy," Bridget, Temple's wife blurts out at him. They had been run off his new Massachusetts farm that they had recently bought before the start of the war. She had been an Irish servant who had abandoned her master to marry Joshua Temple. He was her only family in this country, so she aided him in this battle.

"If the supply sergeant would get us some fresh meat from the farms across the river, you will eat good," Bridget said. "Until then this will keep body and soul together," she says as she waves the ladle at Temple threateningly.

Temple didn't want to eat it, but there was no choice. He gulped it down as fast as he could so that he would not have to think about it, or taste it.

"Mr. Temple, Mr. Temple," Toby yelled between exhausted depth breaths. Toby and another drummer boy had run across the top of the drilling field. "We are here for the rest of the story," shouted Toby after he and his black friend caught up to him.

"Who's your friend?" asked Temple.

"I'm Jeremiah Turner," said Toby's friend. "We're both drummers."

"Okay. Go grab a bowl of stew and let's go inside the hut and see if there is any room near the fire," said Temple.

There was one seat near the fireplace and room on the floor for the two boys. Little did Temple realize that he would become the camp entertainment for the young boys, but he relished the idea anyhow.

"So, you want to hear the story about the King Philips War and Captain Benjamin, do you?" Temple asks.

"Yeah, that's what we're here for," they say almost in unison between gulps of the stew.

"It will be a long story and might take a couple of nights," Temple says.

"That's okay, we like it," says Toby as Jeremiah nodded, mouth full of stew.

"Well, it begins with an Indian, of the Wampanoag tribe says Temple. He came running into Governor Josiah Winslow's house with an urgent message. Just like you two guys came running up to me earlier. He lived in Plymouth, which at that time it was a colony that ran from the Ocean, including Cape Cod," he says he raises his arm making a muscle to mimic the form of the cape. It goes to the Sakonnet River about 40 miles away. But what the Indian had to tell the Governor was very important…"

"What was it," Toby blurts out.

"Let me get to it." Don't try to rush the story. "It'll take some patience on your guys part, okay?" says Temple.

"Okay," says Toby as Jeremiah nods again.

"So, this Indian named John Sassamon, that was his Christian name," explains Temple. "He was one of the 'Praying Indians' who were Indians who had become Christians. The Plymouth men took it as their job from God to bring the gospel to the Indians. Sassamon was one of them."

"I thought they were all savages," said Toby.

"Are you both Christian?" Temple asks.

"Yes sir," the boys said in unison.

"It says somewhere in the scriptures, the book of Acts I believe, that says God has made all men of one blood," says Temple. "That makes you two blood brothers. Besides, you'll see how Benjamin Church learns how to fight like an Indian. That's a lesson you boys should learn. You can learn from almost anybody. It's when you think that you know it all that you get in trouble."

As Temple is speaking Simon Peterson, one of the infantrymen walks in and approaches the fire to warm himself up when he sees Jeremiah, looking on him with disdain.

"Who let that negro boy in here?" yells Simon Peterson.

"I did" answers Temple, "and he's staying here."

"Over my dead body," says Peterson.

"Well, that can be arranged, and let's say, no one would miss you," Temple replies, as snickers rise in the room.

"This is a whites only barracks," says Peterson.

"Peterson, who saved your life at Breeds Hill?" asked Temple.

"Breed's Hill, uh I don't remember," Peterson mumbles.

"Was it Salem Poor?" Temple demands.

"Yeah, Salem something," Peterson mumbled in return.

"Who, I couldn't hear you?" Temple says.

"Salem Poor," Peterson mumbled again.

"And he was a big strapping black man named Salem Poor who saved your life and then got bayonetted by the British. Seems to me, you owe your life to a Negro, wouldn't you say so Jeremiah," outrageous catcalling laughter rises up in the background.

Young Jeremiah choked momentarily on a piece of potato and was too scared to answer, as Toby aggressively nods in agreement.

"Anyhow, back to the story," says Temple. "Sassamon goes to Governor Josiah Winslow's house to give him important information. He tells the Governor that the Indian chief, also called a sachem, his Indian name was Metacomet, his English name was Philip, that's where we get the name of the war, King Philip's War. Anyhow, Sassamon tells Governor Winslow that Philip was planning a general war with other tribes against the Englishmen. He also said that he feared for his own life by the mere fact that he was telling the governor this information. Winslow was disturbed by this information, but he didn't know what to do about it. There had always been such rumors and most of them were just empty fears. Still, Sassamon was no ordinary Indian. He was a praying Indian and had lived in one of the Indian villages on the outskirts of the English settlements where the Praying Indians resided. He had risen to the point where he was a leader in their church and would teach at their meetings. Yet, he went back to living with the Wampanoags for some time. Since he knew the English language well, and he could write, he became the official scribe to Philip. Then whenever Philip needed a message sent to the English, he would have Sassamon write it up for him. That way, Sassamon would become aware of any plans, including war that Philip was making plans for. This meant that he had to make a big change again and leave Philip and go live with the Praying Indians and the English. Winslow had a dilemma on his hands. Sassamon was warning of war, but there had been reasons to question his reliability. He had a falling out with Philip at one point, so this might be a personal issue. And the English had gotten caught in the middle of Indian power political wrangling before as well. It's not just Englishmen who have internal political battles. Winslow would have many sleepless nights. But he did nothing with Sassamon's information at that time."

"Unfortunately, Sassamon now had powerful enemies. And a couple months later his dead body was found under the ice, in Assawompsett Pond, his gun and a couple of dead ducks were found on the shore. His body was quickly buried without giving much thought to how he died. But later, when, the circumstances started becoming clearer, his body was exhumed and they noticed that his neck was discolored and bent strangely, as if he had been strangled and then shoved under the ice to hide the murder, to make it look like an accident."

"At first some questioned the accident story," Temple continued. "But then it was remembered that when the body was pulled out of the water, no water drained out of the lungs. If he had drowned, the lungs would have been full of water, they were not. Also, the neck was discolored. There was an investigation into his death, and even Philip voluntarily came and answered all the questions in court. He even stated that since Sassamon was an Indian, this was an Indian affair, Plymouth had no jurisdiction in this case. It was after all part of the agreement between the two peoples that each would decide internal matters in their own manner. But Plymouth was suspicious about the motives behind Sassamon's death, especially since Sassamon had predicted his own death, and said that Philip was planning for a war against the English. If one was true, what about the other? One Indian, Patuckson claimed that Tobias, his son, Wampapaquan, and another Indian Mattashunnamo grabbed Sassamon, twisted his head, breaking his neck, and then threw him under the ice to hide his murder. On the strength of this one witness, and the circumstantial evidence of Sassamon's body, the Plymouth court held a trial. As the trial approached, Tispaquin, the Black Sachem of Nemasket, posted the 100-pound bail for Tobias, the only one of the three held in jail, a lot of money back then, and Tobias went to Philip and told him everything he knew. Philip stayed away from the whole trial, probably fearing he'd be tried next, and marched menacingly around Mount Hope with his warriors, intimidating the people of Swansea. Some people started to say that strange looking Indians were coming into Mount Hope to see Philip. Everyone was on edge. The trial took place, the men were found guilty and hanged, except for Tobias's son. He was on the gallows, the rope was put around his neck, but when the trap door opened and he dropped, the rope came undone and he fell to the ground. Seeing his father and family friend hanging there lifeless, he immediately confessed that the two older men did murder Sassamon, but that he had nothing to do with it. Now, by English tradition, if a man is hung, but the hanging is botched and he doesn't die, well, you're supposed to let him go free. But the English kept Wampapaquan in jail, and when the war started a month later, he was shot."

"So why did the Indians go to war with the English?" Toby asked.

"There were a number of conflicts, Temple replied. One was the two different cultures. The English believed in owning land and establishing a permanent home. The Indians roamed around their area, living near the beach in the summer, going inland during the winter, following the fish runs or the best hunting times in the woods. To them you could no more own land than grab water in your hand. It never crossed their minds. But the Indians started selling their land to the English, only to find that the English developed the open fields into farms and fields that limited their hunting, or their movement. Especially when an English farmer would walk out to some Indians and order them to get off their 'private property' armed with his musket. It was limiting the Indian way of life, but this was the English way of life. Since the Pequot War in 1637, the English had become the ultimate powerbrokers in New England. Then in early 1662 the English had another of the many war scares that centered around Wamsutta, the sachem, king of the Wampanoags also known as Alexander. He was Philip's older brother, and he was suspected of allying with Narragansetts to fight the English. The Narragansetts were a powerful Indian tribe in the western part of Rhode Island who could raise a large number of warriors. Winslow at this time was the commander-in-chief of the Colonial Military Forces and he did react, he took 20 men out to bring Alexander to court in Plymouth to answer questions about his actions. The Englishmen found him at a fishing camp and attempted to arrest him and bring him in for questioning. There was a furious argument, and then Sassamon, once again in the thick of things, convinced Alexander to go to Plymouth with them. Once at Plymouth the Englishmen seemed satisfied with what Alexander had told them, but they had demanded to confiscate their guns. That night Alexander developed some sort of illness and on his return to his village, he died. Many Indians, including Philip thought that the Englishmen had poisoned Alexander. This did much to 'poison' the feelings between the Wampanoags and the English which were already turning sour. If the Indians were not itching for a fight before this time, now they definitely were. It is hard to tell what caused his death. Did he have a heart attack, did he eat some bad food, did his appendix burst? No one really knows. But the English had been pressuring the Indians, and the Wampanoags were extremely suspicious. You must realize that life had been changing for the Indians since Europeans first started fishing off of the shores here. The Indians and the fishermen would trade fish or metal tools for the furs that the Indians had. A lively trade business was started that was agreeable to both sides. The problem for the Indians was that they had never had small pox, measles and the flu. These diseases tore through the Indian tribes and decimated the their populations. In fact, you know about the Pilgrims landing at Plymouth Rock, right? Well, the former village that they found and lived in was perfect for them. The land was cleared, there was a good stream running nearby for water, a perfect place for them to build their own village. It had been the village site of a tribe related to the Wampanoag's who had completely died off from disease. So, the Pilgrims took over the spot. In fact, the Indians all thought that the ground was cursed somehow due to the disease and wouldn't attack the Pilgrims because of it. Anyhow, I am getting side tracked. The Wampanoags also were affected by the disease, but not as badly as this other tribe, but it had reduced their numbers. This weakened them against other tribes, like the Narragansetts who might exploit their weakness, attack them, kill off all of their men, take their women and their land for their own. When the Pilgrims proved that they could survive for a while, the Wampanoags made friends with them. They had a strength that the Indians did not, they had plenty of guns, if not plenty of warriors. So, with the pilgrims as allies of the Wampanoags, Massasoit, the sachem was able to regain his position as a powerful leader in the area. The Indians and the Pilgrims traded fairly well, even though they were very strange to each other. But they were able to live side by side. Years go by, then decades, Massasoit dies, Alexander becomes sachem, but all the time the Englishmen keep growing and growing. Some by families having a lot of kids, but also thousands coming by boat from England. Plymouth gets overshadowed by Boston because its harbors are naturally better, deeper, so they are able to handle more trade with Europe. Also, a lot of business, money is transacted there and it becomes its own colony. Always, there is an insatiable thirst, a deep hunger for land to develop into farms and towns. All of this is encroaching on and pushing the Indians out of their homeland or their hunting and fishing grounds. Now granted, the English were buying the land from the Indians, which in the mind of the English is perfectly legitimate and should leave no ill feeling, but the result is the same. The English were buying and developing the land which left less land for the Wampanoags and other tribes to hunt, fish, and move around in. It was destroying the Indian way of life and many of them resented it and wished for a return to the way things were before."

"Then you add in that because of superior weapons," Temple said "the English became the regional power, and at times the ruling body in disputes, which the Indians did not always agree with; so, with distrust and animosity building, a clash of cultures, the mysterious death of their leader after he had been arrested by the English, and then you had a war break out."

"Now the rumors were that Philip, or Alexander before him were trying to unite the Indians, the Wampanoags with the Narragansetts, and the Nipmucks and others against the English to drive them out," according to Temple. "This was the great fear of the English. It had happened to the settlement in Jamestown Virginia in 1622 when one third to one fourth of the population was killed in an attack by the Powhatan tribes. Whether or not Alexander or Philip tried to do this is arguable, it does not seem like Philip was successful at bring a coordinated attack at the start of the war, but many tribes took advantage of the situation once the war had started and joined the battle. No sooner had Philip escaped the clutches of the Plymouth army than the Nipmucks were attacking. The Narragansetts seemed to be sitting on the fence until the English pushed them over it as a preemptive attack on them in the Great Swamp Fight. Once the war had started, it was a dam breaking with cascading water enveloping and destroying everything that was in its way."

"Okay, time for you boys to hit the hay," said Temple.
"Ohhh, do we have too?" They both replied.
"Yes, that's an order, now get. There will be more tomorrow night," Temple commanded.
The boys disappointedly complied.

CHAPTER THREE

The War begins

King Philip. Connecticut history.org

The next night, after all the drilling and the weak excuse for dinner, four boys came to hear about the King Philip's War. Toby, Jeremiah, and Timmy and Josiah.
"Looks like story hour is taking over," here Smith grumbled.
"Not just a story, it's our history," Temple replies.

"His Story," Toby chirps in. "When are you going to tell us about Captain Church?"

Captain Church, okay, well his story begins on his farm," says Temple. "But I am going to be giving you a lot of information about how this war started, so listen-up. About a year before the war with the Indians began, Church had bought a piece of property in a place we called Little Compton. It was surrounded by the Sakonnet Indian land, so he made of a point of getting along with his neighbors."

"You mean the Indians," Timmy asked.

"Yes, of course," It is always good to have good relations with your neighbors. Isn't that right Smithie," Temple taunts Smith.

"You're daft," says Smith. "I never liked any of my neighbors. Always wanting something, bothering me while I'm trying to get work done."

"Okay," Temple says to the boys," remind me not to move in next to his farm. Anyhow, Church is clearing his land, putting up his barn, making plans for his house where he and his wife, Alice, and his toddler will live. He said 'My head and hands were full about settling a new plantation.' One day he gets invited to speak with the lady chief of the Sakonnets, whose name was Awashonks."

"Awasha-what," Toby repeats as the boys laugh.

"Awash-onks, says Temple, live in New England for a while and you'll find a lot of Indian names that are hard to pronounce. Like Quahog or Mattapoisett. So Awashonks was the queen of the Sakonnets, a sachem, that means leader. Church goes to talk to her and she asks Church what he knows about the rumors of war with Philip of the Wampanoags. He was the ruling sachem, King over the Wampanoags which included the Pocassets and the Sakonnets."

"That's getting confusing," said Josiah.

"Well, think of it like this. At the time of the war, you had King Charles of England." He ruled over England, Scotland, Ireland, and theses colonies here in our land. Our land is divided into Massachusetts, Rhode Island, Connecticut…

"New Hampshire New York, Pennsylvania, New Jersey, Delaware, Virginia, North and South Carolina, and Georgia," Toby yells out proudly.

"You forgot Vermont," Smith adds from the background. "Can't leave out the Green Mountain Boys."

"Wouldn't want to do that," says Temple. "They helped Henry Knox take the cannons from Fort Ticonderoga and bring them to Boston, in the snow. Didn't know you were listening."

"Just making sure you get the story right," says Smith, smiling for the first time.

"Yes, now where was I," Temple said, "the colonies yes, even Plymouth at this time was its own colony during the King Philips war. The names change, the land stays the same." Temple says while the boys nod in agreement.

"If King Philip was an Indian, why doesn't he have an Indian name?" asked Timmy.

"He does, it is Metacomet, but he is better known to us as King Philip. Anyhow, Benjamin Church is troubled by Awashonks questions, claims that if there is any trouble, her best bet was to remain friendly to the English in Plymouth, and he made plans right away to head over to Plymouth to find out what was going on. He promised her that he would return as soon as possible with instructions from the governor."

"Before he left, he saw six of the Wampanoag and they had some hard words for him. Church claimed that he told them that they were 'bloody wretches who thirsted after the blood of their English neighbors who had never injured them.' Then he rides off to go to Plymouth and get the story from the governor."

"So, he rides about 40 miles to see Governor Winslow, the same man that Sassamon had spoken to the previous winter," says Temple. " As they are talking word comes to them that there had been an attack on the village of Swansea. It was very close to the Wampanoag home. Swansea is on the mainland of Plymouth that extends into the Mount Hope peninsula where the Wampanoags lived. So, it was no more than a couple of miles them separated from the Indians. If something was happening, they would know about it first, and boy, did they ever."

"The English were scared as they heard the war drums, during their dances and the war hoops around their homes. Many of the homes were far away from any sort of town," Temple reports. "The farms in

Swansea, the first town attacked, were spread out over a wide area. Some of the farmers had abandoned their farms out of fear. That way, in the beginning there was no person to person contact when the attacks began. The powwows, the spiritual men of the Wampanoags, had warned them not to draw first blood of an Englishman. So, at first the attacks were just on the farm animals and the buildings. The Indians set fire to the barns and homes that the English had abandoned, the smoke billowed up into the air for everyone to see. The farmers who were gathered at two garrison houses, Miles to the north and Barnes further east in Mattapoisett could see the smoke. They also sent word to Plymouth for the governor to send armed men out to help the situation as the tensions grew to what looked sure to turn into all-out war."

"This was the worst information that the governor could hear, but things had been building to this point for months, says Temple. "There was no doubt what to do next. He had to summon the militias and send them out to Swansea. This was June 20th, 1675, and Church was still in Plymouth, he hadn't returned to Sakonnet to talk to Awashonks about what the options would be for her and her tribe and he wouldn't have that opportunity for almost a year."

"Philip's men had attacked Swansea and there was no time to be wasted now," Temple reported. "Church immediately reported with the other men to Taunton where the Plymouth men were to wait for more troops to add to the forces. It took a couple days to gather all the men and the supplies that they would need. In the meantime, Winslow ordered the militias of Bridgewater and Taunton to gather about 70 men to send to Swansea. Governor Winslow had immediately written to the Massachusetts Bay colony who responded quickly to muster men to come down and join them. That way they would be able to travel in a large force to put down the uprising. They waited much longer than they had wanted to. On the way there, Church was in the lead, with a bunch of "friend Indians" and they soon outpaced the rest of the army (if you could call it that) they only had a few hundred men. But Church and his Indian friends had killed a deer, cooked and eaten it before the army caught up with them. This showed two problems. One, that Church would have to slow down to wait for the troops, if he were to be in the vanguard, two, the English were extremely slow moving through the woods and encumbered by too many things. In the years since the Pequot War in 1637, the heavy Matchlocks muskets had been replaced by the flintlock though many of the Plymouth men did not get the newer gun. And many of the men carried the European pike, which was great and deadly in the open battlefield set piece battle in Europe. They could be six feet long, they could be ten feet, but they were terrible for trying to maneuver through the thick underbrush of the New England forests. The Indians knew where they were and where they were going at all times. They could run through the underbrush or through the swamps like agile deer. The English were like a huge bull moose, sinking in the muck, getting its horns caught in the vines, moving slow. They were constantly walking into ambushes set up for them by the Indians who would hide in the forest, disguise themselves with tree branches and leaves so that at times the Englishmen only saw the forest shooting at them, but they couldn't see the man with the gun. Eventually the army banned the use of the matchlock and the pike. Everyone had to get a flintlock."

"So, the Plymouth army gets to Tiverton and waits for the Massachusetts men join them. In the distance they could hear gun fire, screaming and yelling, the Indians doing their war hoops."

"As James Cudworth, the commander of the Plymouth army, waited for the forces to build before they moved out, some of the people of Swansea, who had escaped to the Miles garrison decided to venture out on their own and get some of their provisions and belongings that they had left behind in such a hurry. For now, the army was only guarding the garrison. Around June 23rd, at one home, a father and son had gone back only to see Indians ransacking it. The son had a musket with him, and his father told him to use it. He fired at the Indians, mortally wounding one of them. Later another group of Indians approached the Miles garrison. It seems that there was some sort of conference. There is no information that they bore a white truce flag or not, but there was a discussion between the Indians and the English. The Indians wanted to know why the son had shot the one of their men. When they heard him say, "It was no matter," the Indians became furious. The Indians had goaded the English, waited for them to kill a man first, and then all hell broke loose. The war was on. Both the father and the son would soon be killed, but someone sometime was going to draw blood first."

"Then came June 24th ", said Temple. It was a Thursday, a day declared as a colony-wide "Day of Solemn Humiliation Before the Lord" in Plymouth. They prayed about the current dangers they were facing, and for spiritual solutions to their problems. It turned into a day of fear and death in Swansea."

"Major Bradford and Treasurer Constant Southworth were both at Swansea that day," Temple says. "Commander Cudworth was on his way back from a supply mission to Plymouth with 80 additional soldiers. The troops at Swansea were now stationed at three garrison houses, Myles, Brown, and Bourne. At the Bourne house on Mattapoisett some of the English had left the garrison to go gather corn at a deserted farm house, six died there including the boy who fired the first kill shot and his father. Toward the end of the day the Wampanoags came upon a group of people who were coming back from public Worship. One man was killed, others were wounded before they could reach the safety of the garrison. Even the garrisons were not completely safe. One man standing guard at the Miles house was shot dead, two others wounded. There was no doctor in Swansea, so the troops had to send men out to bring a doctor in. They sent two men out, who never made it. Their mutilated bodies were discovered by men sent by the Massachusetts Bay Colony to try to talk to Philip one last time to prevent war from breaking out. They had their answer seeing the lifeless cut-up corpses of the two Englishmen. They would report to the governor of the need for strong military support for the people of Plymouth Colony. On their way back to Boston they ran into another emissary group which had been sent out to speak to the Narragansett Indians. This delegation led by Captain Edward Hutchinson, (son of Anne Hutchinson), would receive a lukewarm assurance from the Narragansetts that they would not help the Wampanoags in their fight. No one in Hutchinson's group really trusted the assurances that the Narragansetts gave. Later, in a town hall meeting in Warwick Rhode Island, in the heart of Narragansett country, it was learned that one of the Narragansett chiefs, Pessacus had warned the English to 'take precautions because he could not control the actions of his warriors.'"

"On June 28th Massachusetts sent a letter to Governor Winthrop of Connecticut informing him of the situation. Winthrop had received the letter by July 1st, along with alarming reports from Stonington and elsewhere along Connecticut's eastern border. They mobilized quickly. Soon, all four new England Colonies where involved in King Philips War" says Temple.

"It is said that one of the Narragansett Sachems had asked why Connecticut and Massachusetts had bothered to get involved in what at first seemed like a local war between Philip and Plymouth," Temple commented. "It went to the cultural difference between the English and the different Indian tribes. The Wampanoags had fought against the Narragansetts, the Narragansetts against the Mohegan, Mohegans against the Pequot, so on and so forth. There was no pan-Indian thinking, though Philip had tried to form one before the war started. He loosely brought the Indians to his case, but the war was not a unified action. It was more like an opportunistic joining by some, like the Nipmucks, and a forced choice by others like the Narragansetts. The English on the other hand were united by their ties to England, though there were power struggles and land rivalries among the different colonies, especially by New York against Connecticut, which explains why New York stayed out of the fight, they weren't concerned about Plymouth's problems. Also, both Connecticut and Massachusetts wanted Rhode Island territory. Still, an attack on one Englishman was an attack on all Englishmen. That was not the case with the Indian tribes. And the Colonies of Connecticut, Plymouth and Massachusetts had joined together in the United Colonies of New England. This union excluded Rhode Island because of animus towards the founder of the state, Roger Williams, the minister who was banished from the Massachusetts Colony over religious doctrinal differences. Rhode Island, (which Roger Williams was still a part of, and he was deeply involved in the peace attempts), they did not send troops. They did however send their ships all over Narragansett Bay and the Sakonnet

River. The Bay and the River forms a "U" shaped body of water with Aquidneck island in the middle of it, and which separated Plymouth Colony from the eastern Narragansett lands and Connecticut. So even though they sent no troops, Rhode Island was deeply involved in the war. And the island of Aquidneck Island in the middle of the state is a large island incorporating Newport and Portsmouth that was a refuge for Englishmen escaping the war. The United Colonies of New England had formed in 1643. It was the result of Connecticut and the Massachusetts Bay colonies sending forces to defeat the Pequots in 1637. Plymouth Colony was supposed to send troops to eastern Connecticut to fight the Pequots also, but they were late to the battle in a quick decisive fight. It is the set piece for the King Philips War in two ways. First it established the concept of a "united" front in case of an Indian uprising in any of the three colonies. The men of Connecticut and Massachusetts along with the Mohegan Indians had trapped the Pequots in their wooden fort, set fire to it and shot at anyone escaping the fire. It was a complete and devastating defeat that destroyed the Pequot domination of Southern New England, established the English as the dominant force, and made the English, at least the Massachusetts Bay and Plymouth colonies complacent about their military prowess. In 1643, the three colonies bonded together in the case of any Indian uprising, which the King Philip's War was the perfect example."

"As for the complacent attitude of their military prowess," Temple continued "at the start of King Philips War, both Plymouth and Massachusetts carried the cumbersome matchlock musket which was not as reliable as the newer flintlock. The matchlock needed a burning "match" a fuse like cord that remained lite while you were engaged in an action compared to the flintlock which struck a piece of flint to create a spark and ignite the powder and the charge in the barrel. The Indians, after seeing the brutal efficiency of the English, bought the more modern flintlocks, gaining the technological advantage thereby. The Indians realized that they could not face the Englishmen in a European style pitched battle in an open field. That was not their style anyhow, so they used their fashion of guerilla warfare to a great effect. They hid in the woods, blending into the background as they ambushed the English. The English had refused to use guerilla styles, considering it to be cowardly and savage. The problem was that it was highly effective. The English would ride in on their horses, making noise as they approached. Obviously, a horse would need to travel on some sort of a trail, which the Indians knew like the back of their hands. Also, even though the English had been in New England for 50 years, they were not comfortable in the woods or forests. The Indians literally lived in the forests when they hunted deer, or beaver etc. They were familiar with how to move, where they were going, and how to find their way around in the woods. The Englishmen got caught up in the vines, tripped over roots and sunk into the mud of swamps that the Indians like to hide in. Not all of the swamps were watery, some were, but they were thick with under growth that made travel by horse useless and gave a great advantage to the Indians. They used camouflage very well, wearing branches and leaves to disguise themselves. So, though the English had a greater population than the Indians, the Indians had a better fighting style."

"Before the emissary mission had returned to Boston, (they had sent riders ahead of them to brief the authorities of their results), two more companies were sent out," said Temple. "One was a company of 100 men, the other a company of mounted troops. They left out of Boston on Saturday June 26th and met the emissary mission on their way back in. There was an ominous sign that occurred that night, a total eclipse of the moon as they marched down to Swansea. They stopped their march and waited for the eclipse to pass, eating whatever food they may have squirreled away. The men's imaginations ran as tried to interpret the eclipse as good news, or bad. They sat waiting for light from the moon to give them guidance again."

"The information from the riders convinced the authorities in Boston that they needed even more soldiers to be sent into the battle," said Temple. "So, on the night of the 26th the drums beat again and another 100 men were assembled. Captain Samuel Moseley was chosen to lead an odd group of apprentices, servants, seamen and some pirates who had been captured by Mosely off the coast of Maine, convicted as pirates, but pardoned to fight the Indians. Moseley was a fearless fighter, competitor, and he hated the Indians with a passion. He would be one of the foremost Englishmen who refused to trust or use friendly Indians as aids or scouts, until late in the war when it was obvious that they were needed, despite what he thought of them."

"Moseley's hatred of all Indians was opposed to what Church wanted to do with the friendly Indians," claimed Temple "and what the Connecticut men did from the start. Connecticut troops worked hand in hand with the Mohegans who had been with both Connecticut and Massachusetts in the Pequot battle in 1637. This hatred and prejudice on the part of the Massachusetts and Plymouth Colonies would prevent the colonies from ending the war in the summer of 1675 and caused misery for many people throughout the war."

"The advanced force had received word that more men were on their way, so they waited at Woodcock's garrison at Attleboro before they moved onwards," said Temple. "When they arrived in Attleboro they proceeded to Swansea, just north of the neck of land that then expanded into the head of the Wampanoag village and Mount Hope which was not a mountain, but more like a tall butte of land of 209 feet that jutted out into Mount Hope Bay and the Narragansett Bay which it was adjacent to."

"In the garrison Captain Cudworth now had a force of 350 Englishmen and the Mohegan Indians against an unknown amount of Wampanoags," stated Temple. "A short distance down the road from the garrison was a bridge that led over a stream and into the Wampanoag area. A dozen of Captain Prentice's men were getting anxious to see some action. Benjamin Church readily agreed to go with them. Quartermaster Joseph Belcher and Corporal John Gill led the men out. They thought that they would be riding for a while, taking a local man by the name of William Hamond as a guide, but they didn't get far before they found some action. Just as they crossed the bridge, they were ambushed by the Wampanoags. Hamond was mortally wounded and slumped in his saddle, barely remaining on top of his horse, Belcher was shot in the leg and had his horse killed underneath him. Corporal John Gill felt a bullet strike him, fortunate that his thick buffalo skin coat and padding saved him from having the musket ball penetrate his body.

Most of the rest of the group turned and galloped back to the garrison house. Church yelled at them to come back and help the wounded, but to no avail. One soldier helped Gill and Church put Hammond onto Gill's horse and got him back to the garrison house where he died of his wounds. Church continued to yell for the troops to come join him to pursue the Indians. It was for naught. No one joined him. He went back to the garrison where the rest of the troops had watch in safety."

"Major Savage finally came that night with his men and supplies," said Temple. "He had further good news that Massachusetts would be sending more supplies via ships to Swansea. Of course, they would have to navigate around Cape Cod across Buzzards Bay and then up the Sakonnet River to Swansea, so they were a few days away from now. But Cudworth was glad to finally have a full force of over 400 men, plus Indians to hunt down Philip. It's not clear who took charge, whether Cudworth or Savage, but it seems like they worked things out."

"The next morning June 30th, was a rainy day," according to Temple. "A large group was sent out after the Indians, but the trail was cold. They fanned out wide to the east and the west and still no Indians, but they saw the blackened shells of the former houses and barns. In their amateur nervousness the only shots fired were cases of friendly fire. Fortunately, the victim, Perez Savage, son of Captain Savage, was only slightly wounded. As they came to the narrowest part of the land between the Kickamuit and Warren Rivers they came upon a grizzly sight. The heads and hands of eight of the Swansea men killed on June 24th. They were on poles stuck upright in the ground. It was as if the Indians wanted them to find this site to inflict fear into them. The Englishmen took them down and buried them. Then they proceeded in formation throughout the peninsula until they came upon the Wampanoag village. The wigwams were still there, so were their drums though they had been staved, and their corn was still in the field. It appeared that they had fled via canoes probably to the Pocasset area where Weetamoo was. Some on the English side viewed this as a great forced evacuation and a success for their side. Church thought better of their situation. As far as he was concerned:

"The enemy were not really been beaten out of Mounthope Neck, tho' 'twas true they fled from thence; yet it was before any pursued them. 'Twas but to strengthen themselves and to gain a more advantageous post. However, some, and not a few pleased themselves with the fancy of a mighty conquest."[1] Church would write many years later.

"The English proceeded to the base of the Peninsula and looked out across the water to Aquidneck Island, Temple continued. "A boat from the town of Portsmouth was there to take them across to dry accommodations on the island. The Massachusetts men stayed in Mount Hope, in the miserable weather, the Plymouth men took up the Rhode Islanders assistance for the night. The next day the leaders were discussing what to do next. Church suggested to sail to the east, to the Pocasset's land and pursue Philip. It was decided to stay and search out all of Mount Hope, (there were rumors of a stone fort somewhere) and it was possible that Philip would try to return to the area for food or provisions or whatever. So, Captain Cudworth decided to build a fort as proof of a great victory and establishment of English control over the area. Captains Moseley and Page where to keep the area under surveillance, and Captains Henchmen and Prentice would patrol the area north of the village in Swansea and Rehoboth. Meanwhile Philip had escaped the clutches of the English and was miles away with Weetamoo and her tribe. Cudworth had prevented Philip from going north it is true, which only left escape by canoe to Pocasset, yet he missed the opportunity to prevent the water escape."

"To muddle things up even further the authorities from Massachusetts were still nervous about the Narragansetts," according to Temple. "On July 5th they sent Captain Edward Hutchinson with a small retinue to speak to the Narragansetts once again. This time they were to get "positive guarantees" from the Narragansett sachems.

---

[1] The History of the King Philips War Volume 1 by Benjamin Church Forgotten Books Page 25

If they did not get these guarantees, then the Massachusetts military was to take action. This meant that the Massachusetts forces would be taken from Swansea and sent to Narragansett country to back-up the delegation. So, the forces that could be used to chase down Philip in the early days of the conflict where drawn away to force the neutrality of the Narragansetts. Unfortunately, the heavy-handed tactics that the Massachusetts authorities were using were pushing those same Indians into Philip's camp."

"The meeting took place on July 8th when the Narragansett sachems showed up with a large following of armed warriors," said Temple. "The English took this as an affront to a peace meeting, but then again, they had Moseley and his men with them as well. The peace negotiations did not fare well, until the Connecticut delegation had shown up on the next day. This after all was an effort by the United Colonies of New England. The Connecticut men pushed for a more conciliatory attitude toward the Indians. They had their own reasons for doing so. Connecticut's eastern towns were sparsely populated and open to attacks by hostile Indians. Secondly, Edmond Andros had been appointed governor of New York in 1674 by James, the Duke of York, prince to the king. Andros renewed the old quarrel between Connecticut and New Amsterdam, now New York over the eastern part of Connecticut from the Connecticut River to the Hudson river. Both New York and Connecticut where claiming control of it, though it was Connecticut settlers who were living there. As the Connecticut delegation reached Warwick for the negotiations with the Narragansetts, Andros had anchored off Saybrook near the mouth of the Connecticut River with two sloops filled with soldiers to claim the territory. So, Connecticut faced the possibility of a two-front war with the Narragansetts and New York, and so they were not in the mood to antagonize the Narragansetts. The situation got so intense that on July 12th, the Connecticut General Court decided to call for the return of Captain Winthrop. Fortunately for the delegation, they did not receive the order in time to disrupt the negotiations. Also, after sitting off Saybrook for four or five days, Andros gave up on his plunder of land, for now. He sailed back to New York. The English and the Indians signed a treaty. In it the sachems agreed to remain loyal to the English, and to treat the Wampanoags as enemies. The English in turn promised to pay for all Wampanoag captives, or heads that they produced. All previous land grants to the English were confirmed, and the Narragansetts were to give over four hostages. It is worth observing that the major sachems were not at the final signing, but secondary, 'councilors' signed for the Narragansetts.

"The 'peace' negotiations were a propaganda win, but a loser on so many fronts," said Temple.

"While the Massachusetts men were negotiating with the Narragansetts the Plymouth men decided to do the same with the Pocassets and the Sakonnets led by the female sachems, Weetamoo and Awashonks, respectively," said Temple. "Little did they know that Philip had already contacted Weetamoo and was hiding in the Pocasset swamps with her and her tribe. The Pocassets would be firmly on his side throughout the war. Awashonks was a different question. Church had promised her that he would return to her to let her know what the Governor (of Plymouth) was planning when the war broke out and he got swept into the militia. So, he relished the idea of visiting either of these tribes, but especially the Sakonnets as both a personal quest, fulfilling a personal promise, and as a military representative. Also, he hated what he considered to be the foolhardy busywork of building forts. It was a waste of time and manpower as far as he was concerned. And considering that Cudworth's slow movement coupled with this busywork, Philip was able to slip out of the grasp of the English time and time again, it was a useless endeavor. Church preferred to be on the move, hunting and chasing, not stationary and building what he considered to be useless forts."

"So, while the Massachusetts men were in Narragansett country, Cudworth went to Plymouth to secure badly needed supplies, Matthew Fuller and Church led an expedition of about 40 men to the other side of the Sakonnet River into the land of the Pocassets and Sakonnets," according to Temple. "When they landed, they split-up again, Fuller going into Pocasset territory, Church led 19 men towards Sakonnet country. Some of the men were itching to see some Indians and get into a fight. Church promised them that soon enough, they would find what they were looking for. But at the start, all the men were finding were rattle snakes which forced them off one of the Indian trails that they were on. So, they went through a field called Pease Field when they spotted two Indians. Church yelled out to them, still thinking that there was a chance for talking, when they ran off into a nearby wooded area. Then the woods opened up with musket fire and musket balls flew all around Church and his men. Fortunately, none found their mark. Church could see the Indians with the guns gleaming in the sunlight moving to encircle his men. The field was close to the shore, so he ordered the men to go down there and to remain in a tight formation for protection. He also told them all to take off their coats so that those on the boats would see their white shirts, showing that they were Englishmen. There were a number of boats sailing in the river for just such a situation. The rocky shore did not give the Englishmen very much shelter. They were outnumbered by about 300 to their 19. The supply of powder was limited, and it was getting late in the day. If night fell upon them before they could be extracted, the Indians would have them and cut them up as they did to the eight men at Swansea. A boat came near the shore but got driven away by the enemy's gunfire. Some of the men wanted to make a break for it into the woods, but Church told them to stay put and close together. Besides the Indians would have their way with anyone who tried to run into the woods. Suddenly a sloop appeared approaching the men from the north, from the direction of Gould Island. As it slowly made its way to the men, they had hope, if their gun powder held out. Finally, it anchored and let out its two-man canoe which drifted to shore. The first two men waded out to bring it close enough to climb in and paddle out to the boat which was receiving and exchanging gunfire. They repeated the scene again and again until Church was the last man that needed to be brought in. Now according to what he wrote in his book, he ran back into the field to grab his hat and his sword which he had placed by a well at the beginning of the fight. If true, it was a foolish move, but he was successful."

"Captain Benjamin wouldn't lie," Jeremiah said defending his newfound hero.

"Did I say he lied, no, no- sometimes the story grows, especially with time," replied Temple.

"Didn't the Indians shoot at him?" asked Toby.

"Yes, they did, but they all missed. So, I guess that proves that God watches over babies, drunkards, and foolish Englishmen," said Temple, as the men in the room chuckle.

"Wow!..." the boys exclaim.

"So anyhow Church gets in the canoe and paddles over to the boat where he greats his good friend Captain Roger Goulding," says Temple. "The fight had lasted from Midday to about dusk. Church's men had used up almost all their powder. It was a close call. So, Church's men reunited with Fuller and return to their base in Portsmouth. When they again meet with the men from Massachusetts, they made plans to attack Philip in force in his Pocasset swamp hideout."

"While this is going on, other Indian tribes are going on the attack. The Nipmucks, from the Worcester area of Massachusetts come down to Mendon, just above Rhode Island killing several people there. Philip's brother-in-law Tispaquin, the Black Sachem attacked Middleboro, Totoson from the Buzzard's Bay area attacked the town of Dartmouth," said Temple

"The full might of Cudworth's forces, all 450 plus Indians marched into the Cedar swamp of the Pocasset tribe looking for Philip and his men. The woods were dense with vines hanging down from branches and undergrowth entangling your feet and weapons. Also, where it was still wet, the English would sink into the mud, but the Indians knew how to maneuver through the areas. Moseley and his men led the forces into the woods. He brought with him his pack of dogs which didn't really make a difference. The Indians were able to pull off a planned retreat from the English through the woods without much of a problem. The English lost eight men and had to give up the chase before it started to get dark when the Indians would be able to prey upon them at will. So, the English withdrew from the woods," Temple said.

"Still the English thought that they had a tactical victory," Temple continues. They figured that they had Philip cornered, and maybe they did. But they then made a foolish blunder. They sent many of the troops home because the fighting was too expensive for the colonies. Captains Savage and Moseley went home with their men. Cudworth stayed with about 200 men which he split up between the fort at Mount Hope, Swansea, and the new location in Pocasset. Also, he sent about 100 men, including Church to Dartmouth to help that town out. So Cudworth built another fort in Pocasset to keep a watch on the Taunton River to prevent Philip from escaping. Yet, Philip and Weetamoo knew the woods immensely better than the English did and were able to sneak out of the Englishmen's watch, ford the river and head north towards Nipmuck country. This was another blind spot of the English. They thought that Philip would go back to Mount Hope because of the corn that was growing there. Instead, they went into the arms of the group of Indians with whom Philip's father had gone to spend his old age."

"Philip and Weetamoo were moving towards the north with about 250 warriors and some of the women and children," Temple recounts. "They had had to part with about 100 of the slower women and children who could not keep pace with the fleeing tribe who probably went to the Narragansett area. These Indians would probably be taken prisoner by the English if they stayed with the warriors. Philip and Weetamoo passed by the village of Rehoboth where they were spotted by one of the villagers. Soon the minister Noah Newman was organizing a band of men to pursue the Indians. A group of 50 Mohegan Indians under the son of Uncas, Oneko, happened to be there as well and joined the pursuit. The English were hoping that Captain Henchman would meet up with them for the battle, but the Rehoboth men could not wait. They struck out after Philip and soon caught him at Nipsachuck in Smithfield Rhode Island. As they scouted the area, they heard someone from Philip's camp chopping wood for camp. Newman's group decided to attack at first light in the morning. When the morning came as Newman's group was getting ready for the attack, a some of Philip's men were foraging for food and stumbled upon the Englishmen. The shooting started and the battle was engaged. It went on for hours and Philips men got the worst of it. Around 9 a.m. the fighting ended when Philip's people were able to disappear into a swamp. Philip lost 23 men, the English only two. But Philip was still hungry and miles away from home, and miles away from Nipmuck territory. Henchman finally joined the forces but waited until after the Mohegans had taken their war trophies of scalps and other plunder from the dead Indians. The next morning Henchman and the English pursued Philip, but they had escaped again. It was another moment when if the English had pressed their advantage, they could have captured Philip and put a quick end to the war. But they did not. Philip escaped to the north, Weetamoo decided to go south to the Narragansett area with the rest of the women and the children. She was hoping that they could find shelter down there, and for a while they did. Philip made it to Nipmuck territory and was well received. Even though he gave the Nipmuck's sachems much of his wampum's belts, a symbol of great wealth and status for the sachems, Philip's role in the rest of the War that is named after him, became secondary, eclipsed by other chiefs and sachems. He had tried to organize an Indian uprising, tried to unite the disparate tribes under him, but generally failed. What he was able to organize was an unorganized war of opportunity by different Indian tribes. They could see that ultimately the English encroachment and growth spelt doom for the Indian way of life. Still, he was not the dynamic force to unite the various tribes into one. Possibly it was not achievable for any one of the sachems to unite people who for millennium had been independent of each other and had warred with each other over that same time. In 1665, ten years before the war Philip had lost the respect of the Wampanoags on Nantucket Island when he tried to force his will upon them. There were about 1500 Wampanoags and maybe 100 Englishmen. One of the Nantucket Wampanoags, John Gibbs had broken a native taboo; he had insulted Philip's father's memory by speaking the name of his deceased father name so Philip went to the island to confront the offender. It was sixty-five miles from Mount Hope by canoe to Nantucket. When he arrived there, they moved along the southern shore and then took Gibbs prisoner. Philip was about to have Gibbs executed when the English, who favored Gibbs, he was a Praying Indian in good standing with them, so they tried to ransom his life. Philip held out for more, but the English could not match the price. So, the execution was on. Then the English threaten Philip saying if he did not immediately leave the island, they would rally the Indians and "fall upon him and cut him off to a man."[2] Though both Philip and the English knew that the threat was hollow, it was Philip who backed down and took the face-saving 11-pound payment for Gibbs. The Nantucket Indians for the most part accepted Christianity as did the Cape Cod Indians. They stayed neutral in the coming war which diminished the influence of Philip and foreshadowed a weak attempt to drive the English out of New England when the war did break out."

"This brings up another cultural point that is important to look at," Temple reports. "When the Englishmen first came to these shores, the Pilgrims, they made their job to convert as many of the Indians, the Wampanoags to Christianity as they could. This was their reason for being, and even the state motto of Massachusetts shows an Indian asking for help, spiritual help from the Pilgrims. It is actually a quote out of Acts 16:9 where the Apostle Paul had a vision of a Macedonian man saying come over and help. So, the Englishmen saw themselves as Apostles bringing the gospel to the Indians. Now, for the most part the Pilgrims and the Indians got along fairly well, except on this point. That is because Massasoit, Philip's father was the Sachem, the leader, spiritually, physically, politically. Christianity actually undercut some of his power, some of his role in his people's lives. If they became Christians, they no longer owed him their fealty, their obligation, to the Sachem. Jesus now became in a way their Sachem. Massasoit might lose tribute, or have fewer men to call out as warriors. It was ultimately a power loss for Massasoit and anyone who followed him. The Indians who lived in Praying Indian villages did not owe their loyalty to the Sachem. But neither did the Englishmen truly accept the converted Wampanoags as one of their own. It was a strange reality that these "Praying Indians" lived in. But Massasoit saw this as a problem, even complained about it to the Pilgrims, but this was the one thing that they would never budge off of. The Pilgrims did not come here to conquer, but to convert. It set-up a culture clash that was part of the

---

[2] Nathaniel Philbrick, Mayflower (New York Viking, 2006), 210

war. But the Nantucket and Cape Cod Wampanoags stayed out of the fight because many of them had converted and this weakened Philip's position in the war."

"Anyhow," Temple says, "that was just a thought that popped into my mind. Now to get on with the story, Philip disappears from the English during August. He might have been sighted near Brookfield. The Connecticut River Valley had several settlements that were days away from the bay colony. There were six settlements, the largest being Springfield, Hadley, Northampton, Hatfield, Deerfield, and Northfield. There were other smaller villages, but those along the Connecticut River were the main towns. These were all in Massachusetts, but because they used the Connecticut River as their source of transportation and communication these people felt more in common with the people of Connecticut. (The river makes a straight North/South course through Massachusetts and Connecticut, emptying in the Long Island Sound.) This would cause a constant source of friction between the two colonies. Connecticut could respond faster with men and material than Massachusetts could, but this was not their responsibility. Also, when the Connecticut troops were stationed in the garrison houses along the Connecticut River, the Connecticut people would complain that their protection was being neglected while Connecticut troops were protecting Massachusetts land. And Massachusetts had to watch its back door as troubles started to brew in Maine, part of its colony just as Connecticut had to keep a wary eye on Governor Andros in New York. This was enough to overwhelm the small colonies of Massachusetts, Plymouth and Connecticut and may be the explanation of some of the many blunders by the United Colonies of New England as the war raged on in their midst."

"The English army had many dilemmas that they were dealing with," says Temple. "One, they could defend the garrison's by their presence there. Two, they could go out in part with the farmers to their fields, providing protection, relatively close to the garrisons, therefore being close enough to provide an adequate guard, or three, they could chase the enemy down and engage them in the field and do battle with them away from the garrisons. All of these options came with risk and reward. The townspeople wanted the protection of a standing army in their town, but the Indians were not going to attack a well-fortified town. So, the town is protected, but the enemy just seeks an easier target. (The local militias were too small to fend off a concerted attack of hundreds of Indians, though the army was made up of those same militia.) To protect workers gathering food from the field was pretty much the same as protecting a garrison, though with some additional risks. How far away would they travel from the garrison, how long would they be out there, how many soldiers would go. The crops/food stores were a stationary object that could be scouted out and set up for a trap by an enemy group. The workers could be still attacked, as well as the garrison. Then there is engaging the enemy in the field, which every red-blooded Englishman wanted to do. The whole English form of war was to engage the enemy in direct combat of multitudes of forces which could lead to a decisive victory or loss. The Indians were not going to do this, though the English would chase the Indians with that hope in mind. These three things, underscores the strength of the Indian position. They had the scouting abilities, the stealth, the cunning to catch the English at their weakest. If the English hid in the garrisons, the Indians could and would burn down the rest of the town. This was not only houses and barns, but granaries, grain mills, sawmills, any building of commerce were the collective work of a community was done. This included killing or stealing livestock. So, an attack on the town, that spared the population, could still wreak havoc on the economic lifestyle of the town. Such was the case in Springfield. If the English went out to gather food or necessities outside of the garrison, then that divided the strength at the garrison and the work place provided two targets to attack. If the army in mass went out into the field, that left the town exposed to attack by the enemy. The whole problem was that the Indians were mobile as a society, and the English were stationary as a society. The whole Indian community could pick up and move in an evening as we saw in Mount Hope when Philip evaded capture by moving his whole clan out of Mount Hope to the Pocasset area. What the English (except for Church) thought was a desperate act of fleeing a greater enemy force was just the agile movement of a mobile people. This agility frustrated and killed many English in the repeated ambushes and surprise attacks by the Indians on the English."

"The flipping of the Springfield Agawam Indians surprised and shocked the people of the Connecticut River Valley," said Temple. The Agawam had been trustworthy and friendly before they attacked Springfield. This change of attitude by the Indians poisoned the minds of many Colonists towards any and all neutral/friendly Indians. It was hard for them not to see all Indians as the enemy. Captain Samuel Moseley hated the Indians, but he had his reasons why. To him they were all untrustworthy and deserving to die, even the Praying Indians that lived among the Massachusetts Bay Colony. This hatred would blind his eyes to the idea that some could be good and useful allies.

"Anyhow," Temple continues "the war has now expanded. Plymouth Colony had failed to contain Philip, he escaped their grasp three times already, and now resided in Nipmuck territory. But he was not the leader of the Indians. Many tribes now took the opportunity to attack the English, punish them for encroaching on their way of life. As one ominous note, that had to have been left by a Praying Indian who could write English, left on a bridge after one of the attacks read:

> "Know by this paper, that the Indians thou has provoked to Wrath and Anger will war this 21 Years if you will. There are many Indians yet. We come 300 at this time. You must consider that the Indians lose nothing but their Life. You must lose your fair Houses and Cattle.[3]"

"Even though Mendon had been attacked and Massachusetts was on a sure war footing, the Authorities in Boston tried to make one last peace gesture to the Nipmuck Indians," Temple continues. "They sent Captain Edward Hutchinson fresh from his success with getting a peace deal with the Narragansetts with 20 men to Brookfield, deep in Nipmuck territory. It was an important stop on the Bay Path from

---

[3] Hubbard History 171

Boston to Springfield. It was about 30 miles east of Springfield and the Connecticut river. Again, the people living in the village, there were about 20 families were totally oblivious to any danger from their neighbors. The villagers were so confident of the friendly nature of the Nipmucks that three of the townsmen, unarmed, joined Hutchinson, merchant Edmund Curtis and a crew of twenty soldiers. Curtis had been to the Nipmuck village previously. The Nipmucks, like the Wampanoags were a group of tribes that in times of peace lived in several distinct tribes, but under one umbrella grouping. Now that war was brewing all the different groups gathered together as one for safety and war plans. That this fact did not alarm the people of Brookfield is curious. But the Indian tribes were nomadic anyhow and would occasionally move the whole tribe to better hunting/fishing grounds, or to shelter against the coming winter. The mere movement of the tribe would not necessarily raise any suspicion on the surface. But now war was near, so was Philip, the instigator of the conflict, and the authorities in Boston needed to know for certain if the Nipmucks would pull back from the edge of war or not."

"Curtis, having the closest relationship with the Nipmucks as a trader went into the village to set-up a meeting with the sachems and Hutchinson," says Temple. "They decided to get together the next day in an early morning meeting at a neutral spot outside of the village. When the appointed hour came and went, the men conferred. The three Indian guides were against going any further, but the local men still thought that the meeting was still a good idea and that if the chief negotiator for Massachusetts himself were to show up in their village, (Hutchinson) there is no way that the Indians could deny the meeting. His mere presence there would ensure things going well. Hutchinson reluctantly agreed. The path that they traveled by was treacherous for the men and their horses. At one point they had to pass a thick swamp to the left and a steep rocky, brush covered hill to the right. The path was narrow, and they had to ride single file through the area. Suddenly the hillside opened-up with musket fire. Instantly they realized the foolishness of the decision, but too late. Hutchinson tried to turn and go back, but the Indians had them cut off. They couldn't go forward because the path was treacherous, to go into the swamp risked drowning, they could only go up the hill through the enemy lines, while being shot at. It was a hard climb. Men were being shot out of their mounts, falling to the ground. Some were only wounded, some were killed. Horses also would be attacked. The screaming and yelling and neighing of the horses must have been unbelievable. But somehow the troop got to the top of the hill after losing eight men, including the three townsmen. Then they had to get back to Brookfield before they Indians cut them off again. Fortunately for the troopers the Indians didn't have horses, so they made it safely to the village, but the Indians were not far behind."

"The soldiers and the townspeople all gathered in one principal house in town the Ayres garrison," Temple reports. "The house was owned by Sergeant John Ayes who was one of the townspeople now lying dead near the swamp heading toward the Nipmuck village. Eighty people were cramped into the domicile, mostly women and children. The wounded were tended to by the women, the men stood by the windows to fire out at the Indians. The leaders of the troops were both members of the wounded from the failed peace negotiations. Hundreds of Indians under the leadership of Muttaump, had surrounded the garrison house and were burning the other houses and barns in the village. Seeing that they could not hold out long in this situation, two of the men Curtis and Henry Young ventured out to try to go get help. They mounted horses and tried to ride out of town but had to turn back. Young would later be mortally wounded standing guard near a window. Another man had tried to go get needed supplies from one of the other houses. He was captured, beheaded and then the Indians kicked his head around for sport in front of the garrison. When they got bored of that they stuck the head on a pole in front of the house, in plain sight for all to see. Curtis tried two more times to get help from Marlborough. The second time, on foot, he was turned back again. Later when it turned dark, he crawled out on his hands and knees and finally broke through the enemy lines to go the thirty miles needed to get to Marlborough. When he arrived, he found that two other travelers had warned the people there of the battle, but he was able to give them detailed information about the fight. While he was trying to bring in help, the Indians had resorted to trying to burn down the garrison house. Some of the Indians would fire flaming arrows onto the roof, but the English would break through and extinguish the flames. Then the Indians piled hay in a corner of the building and set it on fire. The English dashed out of the house and quenched it. The Nipmucks did it again, this time aiming their gun fire on the doors to prevent anyone from dashing out. So, the English broke a hole in the wall, put out the fire and then boarded up the wall again. Then the Indians grabbed a cart loaded it up with hay and other combustible materials. They lit it and rolled it up to the house to burn it to the ground once and for all. Then the heavens broke open with a heavy rain, saving the house. The people thanked God for their deliverance. August fourth dawned, the garrison house had been under siege for 48 hours, but help was on its way. When the two lone travelers had first warned the town of Marlborough, they sent a rider to Lancaster to tell Major Simon Willard and his troops of the dire situation. Willard was on a mission going westward, so another rider was sent out to him to inform him. When the messenger caught up to Willard, he immediately changed his plans and headed to Brookfield. It was a long way to Brookfield, but they covered the distance as quickly as they could. Finally, they arrived, the people of Brookfield had their help. When they got to the town all they had to do was to listen for the war cries and the whooping of the Indians and they saw the garrison house. The Indians were making so much noise that they didn't hear the warning shots of their sentries warning them of incoming English soldiers. The famous preacher of the time Cotton Mather wrote that Willard and his men were able to get to the very door of the garrison before they were spotted by the enemy. So, they were let into the house by their fellow countrymen who gave them 'the most fervent welcome they had ever experienced in their lives.' Also, if the accounts are true, there were several brand-new babies there to greet Willard's troops."

"When the Indians realized that hope of victory was gone with the coming of Willards forces, they disappeared into the forest, but not until they set fire to the remaining abandoned structures. Willard stayed in

Brookfield for a couple of weeks, but it was not worth garrisoning. He and the townspeople abandoned the village," Temple says.

"Next, the Nipmucks attacked Lancaster, killing seven people," Temple reports. "At the time, it was not clear which tribe did the killing and the blame fell on some local friendly Indians, but it later became evident that it was the Nipmucks who had done it. Captains Moseley and Samuel Appleton were patrolling the area. They were then sent on a mission by Boston to find the Penacook tribe and find out where they stood. Wannalancet was the sachem and his father had always advised him to never go to war with the English. The Penacook remained neutral during the whole war and did so by getting out of the field of battle by going north into the upper Merrimack Valley (New Hampshire). But since Moseley was sent to find him and 'talk' to him, and all he found was an abandoned village, he burnt it down. Boston was mad at Moseley for doing so, they wanted this to be a peace mission, but fortunately Wannalancet did not take the bait to go on the warpath."

"So, then Moseley goes and finds the praying Indians who lived in Hassanemesit, near Marlborough," Temple says. "He blamed them for the Lancaster attack, even though they had done no such thing. He took eight to fifteen of the peaceful Indians, the report differs with each telling of it, and then he tied ropes around their necks and marched them off to Boston where they were thrown in jail. Fortunately for them Mr. Elliot, the minister to the Indians who had printed an Indian Bible, and Captain Gookin pleaded for the innocence of the Hassanemesits. They argued so strongly before the council that they did not know what to do. They demurred to Mr. Elliot because he had worked so long at preaching the gospel to the Indians, one of the main reasons that the Pilgrims had given for coming to the "New World," the magistrates would look like complete hypocrites if they harmed innocent people whom they were supposedly trying to bring to Christ. They realized that he was their teacher and trusted his word. As for Captain Gookin, he perplexed the magistrates."

> "But for Captain Gookin why such a wise council as they should be overborne by him cannot be judged otherwise because of his daily troubling them with his impertinences and multitudiness speeches, in so much that it was told him on the bench, by a very worthy person (Captain Oliver) there present that that he ought to be confined among the Indians, than to sit in the bench..."[4]

"So, the magistrates let the Indians out in the dark of the night," reports Temple.

"This so upset the townspeople that they banded together one night in a mob to drag one of the Indians out of the prison to hang him," Temple says. "They stopped at Captain Oliver's house to bring him in on the plan and have him be his leader. Instead of going with them, he beat them with his cane and drove them off. The next morning Oliver told the governor what he had done and the Governor thanked him for his actions. But the people were still angry for someone to kill. They were still angry over Mr. Elliot and Captain Gookin releasing the innocent Indians. But there was one Indian who was scheduled for execution, and the magistrates issued the order to hang him. He was led out to the scaffold to be hanged, but didn't die immediately. His body was dangling and squirming at the end of the rope. Then an Indian came over to his squirming body, took out a knife stabbed him in the heart and drank his blood as he died. When the Indian was asked why he did that, he said 'Me stronger as I was before, me be so strong as me and he too, he be very strong man before he die.'[5] With that the townspeople were satisfied."

"Wow, so why did Moseley arrest innocent men?" asked Toby.

"Yeah, why did the townspeople want to kill them, they didn't do anything to them?" asked Jeremiah.

---

[4] The Old Indian Chronicle Samuel G. Drake page 152
[5] Ibid 153

"Well, boys, war will make you crazy, you will do crazy things sometimes that you wouldn't do otherwise. Some people will go completely berserk out there, and it's good that he is on your side and not against you. Isn't that right Smithie?" said Temple.

Smith just looks at the boys with an evil grin and then laughs a sick laugh, as he rolls over on the floor and then back to his knees.

"Ahh, hahahahahaha. I'll get youuuuuuu. AAOOOuuuuuu. AAOOOOuuuuuu," laughs and howls Smith.

"Okay boys, its best you leave. We get up early tomorrow," Temple says. "More tomorrow night."

The boys slink out staring at Smith who is now howling like a mad dog at the moon.

CHAPTER FOUR

Bloody Creek

Battle at Bloody Creek. Alamy.com

The next day the boys are already in the barracks, as Temple comes in.

"You're late" says Smith. "The boys need their next story." All the boys nod in agreement. There are seven for tonight.

"Really, hello boys, God bless all of you. Okay, where did I leave off?" Temple says as he scrambles for his last place in the tale.

"Mr. Smith was turning into a werewolf," said Toby, as all the boys laugh, and start howling imitating Smith.

"Look what you started," Temple smiled as he remembered last night's departure. "I know where I want to go next. As the war grew, so did the English distrust of the Indians grow, Praying Indian, friendly

Indian, enemy, it didn't matter. It was still only August; the war was only one month into the start of the conflict yet tempers were flaring. The Indians near Hatfield were thought to be neutral, but the people wanted to know. There were many rumors that they were up to no good. This included reports from Mohegans who said that they were acting suspiciously. The Hatfield tribe was related to the Nipmucks, which had just struck Brookfield, so the English wanted to know where they stood, for peace or war and they sent a peace mission. They also demanded that the Indians give up their guns as proof of their neutrality. The Indians procrastinated especially since their livelihood depended so much upon hunting and the gun was so much more efficient than a bow and arrow. Instead, they finally fled to the north by night."

"When they did this, the English sent out troops to hunt them down," Temple goes on. "Captains Thomas Lothrop from Beverly and Richard Beers from Watertown chased after them and caught up to them near Sugarloaf Hill. The Indians fought valiantly, not wanting to be subdued by the English. The Indians killed nine Englishmen before the English backed off. Then the Indians continued their flight to the north. But it was the English who once again drew first blood in this conflict. It is obvious to consider that any hope of neutrality was destroyed by this action. But in the same light, the people of the Connecticut River Valley had good reason to be suspicious. The previous peace mission in Brookfield, led by men who were convinced of Indian neutrality, were killed. Thus, from the English perspective, it was deadly to assume friendship between the peoples. The conflict of a clash of cultures had reached its boiling point, and only one side would win."

"So, where's Captain Church?" Toby asks.

"The Plymouth men aren't in this area. They are in the southeast of Massachusetts. These battles are in the Connecticut River Valley a long way from Plymouth by foot. He'll come back, don't you worry," said Temple as Toby slumps, a little disappointed.

"So, the month of September starts out bad for the Englishmen," Temple recounts. "One man is killed and several houses are burnt in Deerfield on the second day of the month. Then eight men from

Northfield where killed. These were the two northern most towns at the time and it was determined that they were indefensible and that they should be evacuated. On the 3rd Captain Beers and thirty-six men march along the Connecticut River to evacuate Northfield. During their march back with the evacuees the next morning, when they were about two miles from their destination, Beers and company were ambushed. It was a bloody mess. Beers was killed as were more than half of his men. The survivors fled to Hadley and stayed there for the next two days. Then Major Robert Treat, commander of the Connecticut forces in the north, evacuated the garrison house at Northfield. When they were there, they saw a chilling familiar sight, the heads of the English soldiers hoisted on the tops of poles for all to see. This had been done in Swansea, Brookfield, and now here. Over the next couple of weeks more troops arrived to the north of the river valley, including Captain Moseley and his men..."

"Hisss..."Toby utters.

"As I said..." Temple stated while shooting a nasty glare at Toby.

"As I said Mosley's group arrived in the river valley," Temple continued. "Deerfield was attacked and the Indians took a prisoner from there. It was decided to abandon Deerfield as well. Captain Lathrop was ordered to go and get all the people together and load their stuff on carts and then proceeded to go back down to Hadley. They got there in one piece, ordered the evacuation, and then headed south. Once again, the English marched into an ambush. They had gotten about five or six miles south of Deerfield at a place that is now known as 'Bloody Brook.' They had been taken completely by surprise and the fighting was intense. Moseley was in the vicinity and Lathrop's bugler had managed to escape the fight and locate him. Moseley arrived at the battle and engaged with the Indians. Major Treat, at Hadley had also been informed and raced to the scene. When the Indians saw Treat's forces coming, they decided that they had had enough and escaped to the north. After the battle, Moseley retired to Deerfield, Treat took the wounded to Hadley. At night, the Indians taunted the men at Deerfield. The next morning Moseley and his men returned to the sight of the battle and buried 64 men, including Lathrop. A contemporary historian called it the 'saddest day that ever befell New England.' Some of the best New Englanders fell that day."

"How come Moseley is there and not Church?" asked one of the boys.

"Because this is Massachusetts's area, not Plymouth's, Temple replied. "Remember they are two different colonies with different responsibilities. Connecticut is helping out Massachusetts and that is because of the transportation system provided by the Connecticut River. This also causes some contentions that I told you about before. But fortunately for Connecticut, there were no major battles in that state, though there was always the potential for it at any time. So, they are free to help out in the Massachusetts colony or in Plymouth as long as the New York Governor, Andros stays in his state. And don't forget, the three colonies form the United Colonies of New England, so they are obligated to help each other."

"Now, while the army had been fighting in the Connecticut River Valley, the United Colonies Commission had been discussing how to conduct the war," Temple says. " They decided that they needed an army of 1000 men: 158 from Plymouth, Connecticut 315, and Massachusetts 527. There were about 40,000 English, men and women in New England at that time. So, everybody knew someone who was in the fight, father, son, uncle, brother, husband. They also decided that the river valley needed a force of 500 men, 200 coming from Connecticut, 300 from Massachusetts."

"October didn't get any better," Temple recounts. "On the 4th the troops left the major town of Springfield, on the Connecticut river, and bordering the state itself. They were going to march north up to Hadley to chase the Indians up there. The Indians that were around Springfield were thought to be friendly. Even after a grinding mill had been burnt down, the local English blamed it on other Indians, not their friendly Agawam neighbors. Well, once the troops left there was a report that the local Indians were planning something with Philip's men. The information was sent to Hadley, where the forces were. Also, Springfield sent a small group of men, first thing in the morning, led by Lieutenant Thomas Cooper and Constable Constance Miller go to investigate the situation. They wanted to be able to prove the information was wrong, just war time rumors, unfortunately for this small group it was very true. Before they made it to the Indian village, they were fired upon, the constable died at the site, Cooper was able to ride back and with his last dying breath, warned the people of Springfield."

"Soon after being warned by Cooper, the Indians arrive for the attack," says Temple. "Fortunately for the English they were already in or near their garrison houses. There were about 500 people in Springfield, so there had to be more than a few garrisons. The Agawam, led by their chief Wequogan did not attack the garrison houses, but just burnt down the abandoned ones. The smoke filled the sky with ominous grey billows and the fiery sparks flew everywhere."

"Meanwhile Springfield merchant John Pynchon and Captain Samuel Appleton were heading south with 200 men from Hadley, and Major Treat was coming in from Westfield, about ten miles away," says Temple. "His problem was how to ford the wide Connecticut River, they didn't have any boats. Only one small group of men were able to get to the Springfield side. The rest had to watch the destruction of Springfield from the western shore of the river. Pynchon had raced down and arrived to see his town destroyed and still smoldering, he got there early in the afternoon, about 2:00. Around thirty homes and barns were burnt, dozens of families displaced. Yet they were fortunate that because of the warning, only three people died, Cooper, Constable Miller and one unfortunate woman. A couple of others received wounds. Upon the arrival of Pynchon and his 200 men, the Indians escaped into the woods.

"Finally, around the 19th, the English have some luck, but it was hard fought. Luck it came with a price. It was around Hatfield; Moseley and his men were there…" Temple speaks as he is interrupted.

"Booo" sounds Toby.

"'Quiet boy!' Temple scolds his star pupil. "Let me tell the story. So, Moseley and his men see smoke rising above the horizon, and he sends ten men to investigate. Well, you may know how this part of the story goes. Ten went out, only two return. Moseley quickly has reinforcements come in from Hadley and Northampton, so that by the time that the Indians do attack, there is a sufficient force waiting to repel them. A vicious fight breaks out, both sides lose men, but the English gave to the Indians as good as they got. The Indians slunk off into the woods having been bested in this fight."

"The month sees some more minor fights, but for the most part, the Connecticut River Valley quiets down for a while," says Temple. "But this is a good time to break off. Roll call comes early, get to your bunks. You don't want Von Steuben chasing after you with his lash tomorrow, do you?"

"No sir! Mr. Temple." Toby shouts out.

"No sir Mr. Temple," the other drummer boys respond as if he were their captain. Then they all line up marching out to their respective huts imitating Von Steuben. "Eins, zwei, drei, march, eins zwei, drei Marsch…."

CHAPTER FIVE

The Captivity of Mary Rowlandson

audioBoom

All the boys had assembled to hear Temple talk about the King Philips war. The group had grown so large that some of the men in the barracks had started to complain, there were 10 boys squeezed into the hut that night plus the 11 men and Bridget. No more room. But when word had gotten around of what a moral boost it was becoming, Temple drew the interest of some officers, which made him chuckle at the thought.

"Well, I am sure that Toby has told you all about the Great Swamp Fight, so I won't go into detail on that battle tonight," said Temple. It drew disappointed groans. "Just know, that as cold as it gets here, those guys had it even worse, but they pulled through it. It was a bold and audacious strike though. It was risky because they would bring in a large group of warriors into the fight if they attacked. But if they waited, those same warriors would be able to attack them next spring or summer when they could easily hide in the woods and attack the Englishmen at their will. So, because the English feared that the Narragansetts would sooner or later attack them, they attacked first. The Great Swamp Battle happened on December 19th 1675. It lasted for about two hours and it was pretty much all that was important in December and January by the either side's army. In January Winslow, the Commander-in-Chief of the Plymouth forces at that time, attempted to follow-up on the victory but was once again chasing ghosts through the woods of the Narragansett areas. The English were constantly hounding the Indians, but the natives always stayed one step ahead. There were small skirmishes, Winslow would kill a few of the Indians, but the main body always escaped. At the Great Swamp Fight, the Indians had a fixed position that they had to hold. Being chased out it was a great defeat. That was what the English were used to dealing with in their preferred method of warfare. An army coming up to a defended place and the army lays siege to it. The English understood this. When the Narragansetts where chased out, although, physically it was a terrible situation for them, they actually had the tactical advantage again, because more than six months into the war, the English still did not know how to fight in the woods."

"Captain Benjamin Church makes a comeback here for a while..." says Temple.

"Yeaaaa" shouts Toby and the boys.

"He had been convalescing in Newport after the nasty leg wound, he had received in the Narragansett fight, but it wasn't completely healed," said Temple. "One bullet had hit his upper thigh and glanced off of his hipbone. He needed help getting onto his horse and it was still sort of an open wound. But the attempts to corner the Narragansetts now were futile, the men were hungry, almost starving, some were disserting, so Winslow marches them back to Boston, realizing that they had done the best that they could for the time being."

"Now there is something that happened in January, that is extremely interesting, but that doesn't involve the English army," says Temple.

"No??? What is it?" asked Toby.

"I'm going to tell ya," says Temple. "In January, 1676, Philip led a group of his men to New York to talk with the Mohawks. They were a large tribe well to the west, very much feared by all the natives, but Philip figures that if he could get them on his side it would help out the Indian cause greatly. Never mind that that would bring all of New York state and all of Governor Andros' men into the battle as well, something that Connecticut would fear because who knows what Connecticut lands he might try to annex, but that is not something that concerned Philip. So, he treks across Massachusetts avoiding any contact with the English around the Connecticut River Valley and manages to get to Mohawk country. Remember now, that the Mohawks were ferocious and not a tribe to be trifled with. Also, they were an enemy of the Wampanoags, and they had good relations with Governor Andros and the English. They may not have been the least bit interested in a war with the English. Especially for lands that were relatively distant from them. Now according to one historian, the Reverend Cotton Mather, Philip knew that convincing the Mohawks into war with the English would be a hard sell, so he decided to sweeten the pot, so to speak. He came upon a group of four or five Mohawks, he and his men, and killed them, or so they thought. Then he continued to on his journey to speak to the Sachems of the Mohawk tribe. Unfortunately for Philip, one of the men had survived the attack, knew the short cut to the camp, and was able to tell the Mohawks the real story before Philip got there. Needless to say, they were not welcome and were driven off by the Mohawks after a bitter fight. Like I said, only Mather has spoken about that particular incident, but Philip did go to the Mohawks and was sent packing by them one way or another. So, the war stayed confined to New England. The English were doing better, but they were still confounded by the Indian style of warfare."

"Then there is the story of Joshua Tefft" Temple says. "He seems to have been a rebel's rebel. Always getting in trouble as a youngster, always aggravating the preacher and the elders.

"Oh, you mean like Toby," Jeremiah says. Toby gives him a good shove, for saying so.

"No, much worse, why Toby is a choirboy compared to Tefft," said Temple. "Tefft hated everything and everybody, he hated his father, the English, the Preacher, everyone. So, he became a renegade, he went to the natives to live with them."

"No, why would he do that?" asks Jeremiah.

"We will never know," said Temple. "Some people will switch because they were kidnapped while young, and they don't remember anything of their previous life. Some people rebel against civilization. There was one group of Englishmen who tried to found a plantation like Plymouth, not many years after the Pilgrims had settled on the coast who rejected all sorts of common rules of God. They did not have the discipline to survive like the Pilgrims did and either starved, became slaves to the Indians or came to the Pilgrims and begged for forgiveness and food. So, you get all kinds in these woods."

"Anyhow," Temple continues, "Tefft was captured with a group of Indians while they were trying to steal some cattle near Providence Rhode Island. He was brought into the town and interrogated. Since he lived with the Indians, he was in the Narragansett's fort during the Great Swamp Fight, and fled with his master before the place was burnt to the ground. He said that the Indians had come back the next day to assess the damage. He claimed that they found 97 dead and 48 wounded. The usual numbers of dead Indians were around 150 to 200 dead according to English reports, with hundreds of women and children and old people killed in the fire. Tefft also claimed that the fight would have gone so much better for the English if the Mohegans had not shot up into the air in order to miss killing other Indians. This report was taken by many, like Moseley, that the Indian allies, either Praying Indians, or the Mohegans were untrustworthy allies. Others like Church would argue fiercely the opposite. But Tefft's testimony stood out there for people to accept or reject, depending on your disposition. He was hanged as a traitor."

"Eugggggggg," Toby groaned with his head crocked to one side imitating a hanging.

"Yes, dead as a tombstone," Temple stated.

"Now speaking of captives, there is one story that I must acquaint you with," Temple states. "That is the story of the captivity of Mrs. Mary Rowlandson, the wife of Reverend Joseph Rowlandson."

"Uugghh. What about Captain Benjamin," the boys demand.

"We'll get to him later, and I know some of you boys aren't interested in girls, yet, and you just want to hear about battles and fights, but this story is one of the main reasons we fight," Temple says. "To preserve our way of life. And I noticed a couple of you boys spending some time with the washer girls out at the edge of the camp, ehh Joshua, and you Zeke. What are the names of your girlfriends? We're in German country, 'sprechen sie deutsch…' Temple teases a couple of the older boys who have been flirting with local girls as the rest of the boys yell out cat-calls and pick on the two Romeos.

"Okay, listen-up!" Temple demands getting control of the room. "Let me tell you a reality. Sometimes in battle you don't always win. Sometimes the enemy gets the best of you. And this story is one of those situations. There was an attack on Lancaster Massachusetts, actually there were a couple of attacks. The first one killed seven men out in the fields. They were in the northern part of Nipmuck territory, not far from the supply station in Marlborough, but not close either. Then on February twentieth, the Indians attacked Lancaster, there were a couple of garrison houses in the town and most of them survived unscathed, but one, the Reverend Rowlandson's house was overwhelmed. Now Reverend Rowlandson was days away in Boston seeking additional military help for the town because of their situation. In fact, it turns out that two 'Praying Indians' who had been used as spies in the Nipmuck tribes had uncovered a plot by the Indians to attack Lancaster, Groton Sudbury, and Marlborough, which the Magistrates took lightly even though they had sent these two Indians out as spies. They had informed the Magistrates two weeks before the Lancaster attack… the Magistrates did nothing. They had proper information but decided not to believe these Indians, their people. It's hard to fathom. Anyhow, according to Mary Rowlandson's account in her book she said that they came about sunrise, the people in her house heard the gunfire and looked out as several houses were already burning. There were five people taken in one house, she said. The mother and father and suckling baby they "knockt on the head" probably using their war club, a two-foot-long piece of hickory with a large stone or metal wedge attached at the tip of it, which did a lot of damage to your head. Others were outside of the garrison as the attack occurred. One Englishmen offered money to the attackers, but they "knockt him in the head," stripped him naked and split open his bowels. Other men ventured out to save their buildings and defend the garrison, but they were shot down. The Indians were burning and destroying as they went and the English were running to get into Rowlandson's garrison house."

"Then the Nipmucks came to the Rowlandson house," Temple says. "Mrs. Rowlandson claims in her book of the ordeal, that it was the 'dolefullest day that mine eyes have ever seen.' The Indians were all around the house. It was on a hill, so some laid low in the grass to fire upon it. Others got into the barn and were firing from there; others were running around it finding whatever shelter they could find to fire from. She claims that the bullets were flying like hail stones coming out of the sky. They were under attack for about two hours according to her reckoning, and then they tried to burn the building down. They brought out flax and hemp from the barn, probably even using the Englishmen's carts which they liked to do and brought the burnable materials up to the side of the house and lit it on fire. One of the men from inside was able to extinguish it, but the Indians lit it again. This time it took, and the building started on fire. Now the people inside the house were desperate. Some of them were dead, or dying, choking on their own blood. They had six 'stout' dogs as Mrs. Rowlandson said, and though usually they were fearless and would chase down any trespassing Indian, this time even they cowered in fear. Mrs. Rowlandson had one of her children in her arms and one of her sister's by the hand and tried to go out the door. They were met by bullets flying thick around them and went back in. She was shot in the side, the youngster in the abdomen. Her sister's son William had a broken leg and when the Indians saw this, they 'knockt' him on the head. When her oldest son told her that William was dead, she said 'Lord let me die with them.' She was shot dead and fell over the threshold."

"Then the Indians came and grabbed those who were still alive," Temple continued. "They were pulling children apart from their mothers. There must have been shouts of agony from people dying, and children being torn away from their mothers, and Indians whooping and hollering and laughing. One of the Indians grabbed Mrs. Rowlandson and pulled her out. She asked him if he was going to kill her, and he replied "If you go willingly, they would not hurt her." As she was being led away, she was able to look at her surroundings. There was a man who had been "chopt" in the head with a hatchet and stripped naked, but he was crawling on his hands and knees trying to get somewhere safe. Before the attack, when she wondered what she might do in this very situation, she would say that she would choose death over captivity, as her sister had. But when faced with the choice, when the Nipmuck grabbed her and she saw his weapon, she changed her mind, she gave in to 'those ravenous beasts' rather than end her days. They removed her from her house. In her book she would speak about the 20 'removes' in three months that she and the Indians made during her captivity. They were always on the move, which is what made it so hard for the English to pin them down. They never stayed in one spot for long."

"During the fight, she, and her child, Sarah, that she held were wounded," said Temple. "There was no medical attention given to either of them except one Englishmen captive had told her to use oak leaves as a bandage. The child was about six years old and the bullet that struck Mrs. Rowlandson in the side had hit the child in the 'bowels,' she said. It survived an amazing nine days with her in the wilderness. When Sarah finally gave up the ghost Mrs. Rowlandson kept her by her side all night long, not wanting to part with her. In the morning, the Indians sent her away to do things for her Master, Quinnapin. In the meantime, they took her dead child from where it lay and buried it. Later they showed her the burial site, but there was nothing to be done. No time to mourn her."

"Of the 37 that had come to the Rowlandson house for safety at the beginning of the attack, one escaped, 12 were killed, and 24 taken into captivity," said Temple. "The irony of the whole situation was that Reverend Rowlandson had traveled to Boston to get more soldiers to come out to Lancaster for its protection. Upon his return, his town was smoldering in ruins and his family was dead or gone."

"The Nipmucks seem to have treated her well, so to speak," said Temple. "At one point they put her and her wounded baby on a horse. But they didn't use saddles, and she wasn't used to riding bareback. She and her child fell off of the horse, which was great amusement for the Indians, though she thought that she was going to die."

"Quinnapin, a Narragansett sachem, was her master," said Temple. "She was sold to him by another Narragansett. Her other daughter Mary was in the same village, but they didn't allow the two to spend much time together. She had a son, Joseph, who was in another village. He was brought to her when his master was out on the raid of Medfield. Joseph asked about his sister Sarah, if she was dead, and told her that he had seen Mary. They spoke for a while and then they had to part."

"The next day after the reunion, the raiding party returned," Temple recounted. "At first Mrs. Rowlandson said that she could hear them a mile away. By way of whooping, they were telling the people in the village how many Englishmen that they had killed, and with every kill, the village would reply with a shout. Mrs. Rowlandson claimed that the very earth shook with their boisterousness. Soon they came into the camp and to the chief Sachem's wigwam to display their trophies, scalps, plunder, Mrs. Rowlandson did not mention any new captives. But one of the Indians did give to her an incredibly special gift, a Bible. This is interesting, because she did not mention if this Indian was a 'Praying Indian,' (those that had been converted to the Christian faith) or just another warrior. But they must have thought of her as a sachem, (a chief) since she was a minister's wife. The two peoples had lived side by side for 50 years and would have had a good working understanding of how each other operated, who was chief, who was important, for in her account there are indications that she, though being a servant, was treated better than other captives. The gift of the Bible is important. At one battle, a Bible is torn and scattered over the grounds for all to see. It was not a farmer's almanac that was torn and strewn on the ground for all to see, it was a Bible. This was a sign that the Indians, 'heathen' as some of the English referred to them were attacking the very foundation of the Englishman's life. They were attacking the Englishman's very reason for being. They were attacking their God. But in this case, the unnamed Indian presented something of honor to her. It is ironic that Mrs. Rowlandson always held an animus toward 'Praying Indians,' even after her captivity was ended. At times she reflects some of the prejudicious' that many Englishmen held, especially after the war broke out. Still, Mrs. Rowlandson was able to comfort some of the English captives by sharing a Bible verse with the others when she could get an opportunity. So, she shows different emotions in an experience of trauma that she endured."

"There was one other woman, Goodwife Ann Joslin, who was treated very badly by the Indians," said Temple. "She desperately wanted to run away and escape her captivity and told Mrs. Rowlandson, who talked her out of it. Mrs. Rowlandson told her that they were 30 miles away from any English town and Goodwife Joslin was 'very big with child.' Obviously, she would not last long in the woods. The preacher's wife shared Psalm 27:32 with her: 'Wait on the Lord, be of good courage, and he shall strengthen thy heart, wait I say on the Lord.' Well Goodwife Joslin did not wait, but instead complained and begged the Indians to let her go back to the English. They finally replied by stripping her naked sung and danced as a group around her and then finally "knockt" her on the head. She was then out of her misery."

"It is interesting to see the Indian movements from Mrs. Rowlandson's view," said Temple. "Because you can see the slowness and the ineptness of the English army. When the Indians moved out, everybody in the tribe moved out. The young, the old, the infirmed, the wounded. They all forded rivers, paddled canoes, trekked through forests, hid in swamps. All these things were impediments and stumbling blocks for the English. One-time Captain Moseley's forces were close to them, but the Indians crossed a river that stopped the English. And since the English had the Indians on the run and cut off their supply of food, the English thought that they would give up due to starvation. Instead, the Indians did not starve because they could forage the forest for ground nuts or even tree bark that they could make a meal out of. It was slim gruel for an army, but it worked."

"Yeah, I think we had some of that bark soup last night," yelled Smith.

"Tasted good didn't it?" quipped Bridget, Temple's wife. All the boys laughed. "And if you don't be quiet, you won't get any more stew either."

Yeah, when you're hungry, really hungry, even oatmeal tastes like a fine dinner," said Temple. "They would even eat horses' hooves."

"The hoof of a horse, yuck," said Toby.

"Yeah, horses' hooves," said Temple.

"That's tomorrow's dinner," Smith taunts.

"That's it, I've had it," Bridget yells. "No more food for you! Mister Smithie."

"Okay, okay," I'm, losing the audience," said Temple. "But you can be so hungry that even a horse's hoof is good food. And Mrs. Rowlandson was so hungry that she stole the hoof right out of the mouth of a baby that was gnawing on it. Now the child couldn't eat it and was just playing with it, but for a minister's wife to be that hungry that she would steal from a baby, that is a hunger that even we don't know."

"Oh yeah, I'll steal the horses hoof out of your mouth," says Smith.

"Yeah, and I'll kick you like a horse, put my horseshoe in your mouth," Temple replies.

The Boy laugh again at the exchange.

"Okay boys, get out of here. Reveille at sun-up," says Temple.

"Yes sir!" they all exclaim with a salute. One of them has his drum and beats a march and they all go out in soldierly order.

"Von Steuben would be proud," Smith says.

"There be no more food for you in the morning," says Bridget to Smith.

"Ah come on, I was only having fun. I love your biscuits and gravy," Smith pleads.

"You'll be lucky to be eating a horse's hoof tomorrow," she says as Temple smiles.

"Well, at least I'll have something," Smith grumbles.

CHAPTER SIX

The Hero Leaves

Indians attack an English village jatticus.wordpress.com

Again, the small 12 by 14 foot hut is invaded by a pack of drummer-boys. Temple has been asked by officers to repeat the story again at the other side of the encampment when he is done here. Temple is pleased, though a little put out, until he sees all the boys waiting to hear the next installment of the story of their new hero. He greats the boys with a friendly:

"Hello boys, ready for the next part?" as he salutes to the men making room for the night's entertainment.

"Yes sir, can't wait," the boys respond.

"Yesterday, we were talking about Mrs. Mary Rowlandson during her captivity," Temple recounted. "I never finished off the story. The story comes to an end after the Indians made their 20th "remove" as Mrs. Rowlandson called their marches. She was ransomed by her husband and her church community. The Indians had brought her into a council where they were discussing her situation. Also, the prospects for the Indians were not looking good in May when they were making this decision, though it was not completely obvious yet. They asked her how much she was worth, and it was a question that perplexed her. She had never put a monetary value to her life before, but she needed to come up with an answer right at that moment. It had to be high enough to impress her captors, but low enough that it could actually be paid. She blurted out twenty English pounds with some tobacco thrown in. The Sachems considered it, and demanded that her husband show up in person to ransom her. It was not a small amount. It would buy a small parcel of land, big enough to build a house on. The negotiations were carried out by John Hoar, with the aid of two Praying Indians, Tom Dublet and Peter Conway who transmitted the demand to the Englishmen back in the Boston area. The Praying Indians made good intermediaries because they spoke both languages fluently, and like Sassamon, who was killed at the beginning of the war, often they could write English. Mrs. Rowlandson was so happy to hear the good news that she would be released soon that she actually held the hands of the Tom and Peter. This was quite something for her, because she was a well-respected woman in her own right. In the English towns, the wife of the preacher would be referred to as Mrs. Rowlandson, of course her husband being Reverend Rowlandson. The other women in town would be referred to as 'Goodwife.'"

"Yeah, like Goodwife Joslin, who got stripped naked, and then had her brains bashed in," Toby blurted out ineloquently.

"Yes Toby, just like Goodwife Joslin," Temple states. "Odd how that fact stuck in your mind. I'm glad you're listening."

The boys started to laugh at him, so he starts to fight with Jeremiah who hits him back.

"Okay, okay settle down, and I'll get on with the story. The reason why I bring this up is that she wasn't like a girl you might see at an Inn serving you your food. She was a special person in town. As a captive she was a mere servant, doing whatever her master demanded of her, and doing the requests of other people in the Indian village. Obviously, like most women, she was good at sowing and knitting things, so the Indians were constantly demanding her to sow them some article of clothing. She must have done this well because she was rewarded with food, and sometimes, English coins. But still, she was serving them. And the Indians treated her well, they didn't abuse her like…"

"Like Goodwife Joslin," Toby yells out.

Now the boys gang-up on Toby, rubbing their knuckles on his head, punching him in the arm.

"Help, me Mr. Temple," Toby yells.

Temple lets the roughhousing go on for minute or so, then he separates the pig-pile, tells everyone to sit down and be quiet. Toby has to straighten out his shirt, he grabs his hat from one of the boys as he shoots him a dirty look.

"So, Toby, are you going to let me finish, said Temple. I'm the storyteller here, not you.

"Yes sir," Toby replies meekly.

"So, where was I?" Temple queried. "Oh yes, Mrs. Rowlandson was so ecstatic, so happy about the news of her possible release that she grabs the hands of Tom and Peter. But she didn't really like the Praying Indians. Like many of the English, they thought poorly of, they distrusted the Praying Indians. They obviously weren't Englishmen, they were Indians, but had become Christians. The Reverend Elliot of baptized most of them. But in her book, aside from treating these two men warmly, she had an animus towards Praying Indians."

This time Toby raises his hand to get Mr. Temple's attention.

"Is there a problem Toby?" Temple asks.

"Yes, what do you mean by 'animals' towards the Indians?" Toby asks.

The boys break out in mocking laughter, "Ahhh, you don't know what it means," shouts Timmy.

"Okay Timmy, what does it mean," asks Temple

He shrugs his shoulders and shakes his head no.

"Animus, a-n-i-m-u-s. It is hatred or hostility toward someone. It's a word I heard some fancy preacher use. He had studied at Cambridge; in England you see. So, it's got to be a good word."

"Boooo England," the boys jeer.

"Why didn't you say so: 'She hates them,'" Smith said.

"Because I'm trying to educate you Smithie," Temple replied. "Maybe you'll learn something."

"No chance of that, he's thick as a mule," someone else yells.

"So how many Storytellers do we have here?" Temple asks, looking around the room with scorn. "Now let me get back to the story. And yes, boo to England. Mrs. Rowlandson seems to have harbored a hatred of Praying Indians. Now it is understandable, she was captured by Indians, her young girl, Sarah, who died in her arms, was killed by them, her sister, nephew, other friends and family members slaughtered right in front of her, it was all a tragic scene. In her book she lists a string of Praying Indians who had done wrong. One Praying Indian had betrayed his own father to the English in order to save himself, she gloried in the hanging of another who was one of the Sudbury fighters, claimed another wore a necklace of English fingers, and she described the war dance done by another Praying Indian before the Sudbury fight. So even though she was a Reverend's wife, she never got over, the tragedy of what happened to her that day. Even years later when she would see a Praying Indian on the streets of Boston, she would shudder. So, you never know."

"But she was reunited with her husband," Temple said. "They gave the Indians their 20 Pounds, some tobacco, and some alcohol. A couple of weeks later she was reunited with her son, Joseph, and then later with her daughter, Mary. She was treated like a queen all over Boston and other places where she went, and about a dozen years later she wrote her book about it. She was the first woman writer in the colonies. Made her a pretty penny."

"So now we'll get back to talking about Benjamin Church," said Temple.

"Yeaaaa!" the boys shout.

"It's about time," one of them says.

Temple had looked away for a moment and didn't know who had been so rude.

"I'll let you get away with that one, but watch it. I run a tight ship here", Temple warns. As Bridget stifles a giggle, looking down. When she looks again at Temple he knowingly smiles and continues. "Anyhow, you might not like what comes up next for our famous Captain Church. It all starts with a meeting back in Plymouth…"

"A Council of War was called for on February 29th at Marshfield a few miles north of Plymouth by the Plymouth Magistrates. Benjamin Church was summoned to show up there to be offered a command. To the dismay of the Magistrates, Church put demands upon the Councilors as well."

Magistrate Winslow gaveled the room to order as he begins to speak to Captain Church:

"Mr. Church, you have been commended by the Council to accept a command of troops to fight against Philip and the savages in this war. We have heard many impressive reports of your courage and daring, and some of us have seen you in action. We have decided to offer a high position to you. We would like to have you lead a troop of 60 or 70 men to cover the outer towns of Rehoboth and Swansea. You would be responsible to defend those towns, build forts or fortify garrison houses where needed, and aid any civilians fleeing said towns or any others in the area, and be ready at a moment's notice to hunt down and kill Philip," Winslow stated.

Church who has been standing listening to the Magistrate looks down at the ground, gathers his thoughts, and then replies:

"Honorable sirs;" Church answers, "I thank you very much for the honor of being given the opportunity to defend the Colony towns of Rehoboth and Swansea. But there is a problem with what you are saying to me today. A troop of 60 or 70 men is not a strong enough force to defeat the enemy. It has been reported that the enemy is showing up with forces of 200-300 men. They would eat up the small force that you propose. And I believe that it is a huge mistake to be building forts instead of pursuing the enemy when you have engaged with them. Quite often I have been with other commanders, brave men all, but they broke off pursuit of the enemy to build forts. The forts use up precious manpower, are militarily useless against a mobile force like Philip's men, and they become tempting targets to be burnt. But most importantly while we build these useless edifices, the enemy slips through our grip and lives on to fight again."

"So, what do you propose Mr. Church?" Winslow grumbles and the other magistrates stare in disbelief at Church's forwardness.

"Well, since the next time that Philip attacks again, it will probably be in a large force," said Church. "So, your small group of 70 men will be swiftly killed, more farms and houses burned, civilians scalped or taken as captives. You are going to have to meet their force with an equal or greater force. I propose a Colonial troop of 300 Englishmen and 150 Praying Indians."

"Ridiculous! Absurd!" All the Magistrates shout.

"You want to arm the savages and have them fight with our troops!!??" Magistrate Oliver bellows out over the others.

"Yes," replies Church. "That is just what I propose. Look at the Connecticut men. They are fighting alongside of the Mohegans and they are losing fewer men than we are."

"That is different," says Winslow. "They have had a pact with them since the Pequot War over thirty years ago. We can't just can't trust these savages."

"Savages?" Church questions the Magistrates. "I thought they were Christian Indians sir. Didn't Magistrate Elliot baptize over half of Hassanemesit?"

The Magistrates all start yelling at once at this insolent fellow. Winslow bangs his gavel, shouting for order over the raucous crowd.

"What do we need this ingrate for, God will fight for us!" Magistrate Oliver boasted.

"Hear, Hear! Hear, hear!" they all reply.

"I will remind you Mr. Church of who you are speaking to," demands Winslow. "These are the elders of the church and the government."

"Yes, your honor," said Church. "But you have also sent fellow Christians, these savages as you are now calling them, sent them to their deaths on slave ships, or to die on Deer Island. You have alienated possible allies by doing the same, and made enemies of those who might have fought for you."

Pandemonium breaks out as all sorts of insults are hurled at Church. Magistrate Winslow bangs on his desk with his gavel for what seems like minutes.

"Order, I will have order in this council."

Winslow glares at his councilors but saves the most hating stares for Church.

"Mr. Church," Winslow says, barely able to hold back his rage. "We invited you here to offer you a high command. You have responded with insolence and condemnation. Besides, we cannot afford what you are speaking of. This would destroy this community financially."

"Then Philip will destroy this community militarily, and drive you back into the sea," Church responds with disdain.

"You defeatist ingrate!" Magistrate Oliver shouts.

"Throw him out!" is shouted out by most of the Magistrates.

"You say that God is on your side, is he?" Church dares to ask the magistrates. "King David would have recognized what I am saying, he would agree with me."

Now all the Magistrates are fighting mad and shouting invective and damnation on Church.

Magistrate Winslow almost broke his gavel as he tries to bring order to the court.

"You dare compare yourself to David," Magistrate Winslow growls. "You are coming near to blasphemy young man. You are not a pastor, nor a preacher, you are not going to talk to us of the scriptures!" demands Winslow.

Church, realizing he had pushed his luck way too far decided to back down a little.

"I apologize good sirs; I have been too long living with soldiers and have picked up their bad habits. But I truly fear that your responses to Philip's attacks are too weak. What you propose is suicidal. I have plans to leave the country and live temporarily on Aquidneck Island. I will be at Major Sanford's house in Portsmouth. When you need my services, you can contact me there."

"You're going to Rhode Island? Good! That is where heretics, pirates and Quakers live. It's the right place for you," Magistrate Oliver says.

Uproarious laughter fills the room.

Magistrate Winslow bangs the gavel repeatedly.

"Very good, Mr. Church. If we decide we need your services, we will contact you. You are free to go," Winslow says. Winslow bangs the gavel again. "Gentlemen," he says to the other Magistrates, "we need to meet privately and talk."

Magistrate Southworth just sits in his seat, head in his hands.

"Southworth, are you coming?" asks Winslow.

"I can't believe that I allowed my daughter to marry him. He is my son-in-law," Southworth laments.

Back in the hut Temple stops talking for a second. He pulls his knife out and stirs the fire with it. Then he stands up and looks around the room. All the boys are stunned. It is as if they followed some great leader into battle and he turned and fled. Some of them almost had tears in their eyes. They were expecting to hear feats of great daring and accomplishment from their newfound hero, and had their hearts torn out.

"Well, did you want him to lead men into battle and die in a futile attempt to save a worthless fort?" Temple asks. "Don't worry, Church will be back. But what Church was saying was right. The tactics that the English were using were all wrong. They were marching in formation with their fancy clothes and bright shiny buttons and buckles. They got rid of the matchlocks and the pikes and started using the flintlock, to a man. It was a better weapon. Amazing that the people who had knowledge and easy access to buying the best weapons stuck so long with the weapons that had won the last war 30 years before. The 'savages' had advanced their tactics, the English were fighting a bush war with the idea that they were still in Oliver Cromwell's army, marching through the parade grounds at Mayfair in England. They were in the forests of New England. The Indians had purchased the best muskets from the Dutch, or the French in Canada. The Indians would hide behind trees, behind bushes, they would lay low on the ground. They wore branches and leaves as their clothing to hide themselves. The English could only see the forest firing at them. And, the English would march in formation on a road, or single file down an Indian path. The Indians hiding in the woods could see the English, or even hear them from a mile off. The Indians knew where and when the English were going to attack. That is why they were able to lay so many ambushes for them and kill so many of their soldiers. Then they could go rampage and burn a town down. It is not so different from how the German tribesmen were able to beat the Roman Legions at Teutoburg Forest. Moseley, Churches nemesis, even though they were on the same side is a good point. At the Battle of Bloody Brook, the Indians ambushed Captain Lathrop who was leading the people of Deerfield to Northampton. Moseley was made aware of the situation and bravely, yes, I said bravely, he was despicable, but brave, led his men to the battle. According to Hubbard's account of the situation, Moseley had his men keeping formation as they were battling the Indians who were hiding in the woods. If it wasn't for Major Treat, who was at Hadley coming to the aid of Moseley, his command may have been wiped out. Moseley had to bury 64 English bodies the next day, including Captain Lathrop."

"Church not only wanted to fight with the Indians at his side, he wanted to learn from them, to fight like them," said Temple. "Because even as late as February, the war was any man's war. The English scored a big victory in Narragansett, but that was because the Narragansetts had a fixed object, a fort for the English to attack. That is the way the English liked it. They did not like chasing the Indians through swamps, or across rivers. They wanted the Indians to come out and meet them eye to eye on a flat battlefield like armies did in Europe, but that is not what the Indians were going to do. They knew that they could not win in that style, so they used what they were familiar with, their hunting style. Except, instead of hunting deer, now they were hunting Englishmen. And they were able to sneak up on them, or wait for them to come marching through, and then spring the trap. And they were able to win again, and again and again. Church wanted to change that, but nobody would let him. So, he would have to wait for the Magistrates, and the captains and the commanders to realize that Church was right. Otherwise, as he told the Magistrates, it was suicide. And the English wanted to continue committing suicide for another couple of months, until it dawned on them, to use the friendly Indians, the Praying Indians as scouts, and sometimes as combatants alongside of the English. Then the English would start having victories in the field. But don't you worry, boys, Church will be back. He even told his wife so when he was trying to convince her to go to Aquidneck Island.

"They were discussing, achhhemm," Temple clears his throat and looks at his wife Bridget who just looks back with a slight smirk and arms crossed standing behind the boys," as Temple recounts the conversation between Church and his wife.

"But Benjamin," Alice Church pleads, "Plymouth is so far away from the battles, I and young Thomas will be safe there. The Magistrates have promised me. The Clark house is a strong garrison, nothing can happen," Church's wife says.

"Ahhh, you trust these fools too much. Plymouth is the town that sent those 82 Indians into slavery who surrendered to Praying John. They were promised freedom if they surrendered. Especially if some of them would fight with us. No, those fools could have ended the war already. More friendly Indians would have come to our side if they had listened to Elliot, and Gookin, and myself. Now the war is deeper and longer," Church said.

"But I know no one in Rhode Island…" Alice complains.

"You've met a few," Church said. "Anyhow, the Indians know my name and my face here in Plymouth. If they learn that you, my lovely wife and son are hiding in Plymouth, they will double their efforts to take that garrison no matter how many brigades protect it. Then they will scalp your beautiful brown hair and do…unspeakable things to you before they kill you, or they will capture you like Mrs. Rowlandson.… the Indians are smarter and stealthier than these fools imagine. Bloodlust fills even good Christian men and blinds their thinking. No, you must go to Rhode Island. The Sakonnet River protects you from attack on the east, the Narragansett Bay on the west. You will be safe on that island."

"But Benjamin…" Alice pleads.

"You know that I was at the battle in the Narragansett Swamp," Church confesses. "I got shot, but I still argued with the General not to burn the fort. We could have stayed there days, or weeks and had reinforcements escort us out after a great victory. There was food there, it was warm. But no, it had to be burnt, they had to destroy it. Women and children who hid in the wigwams…they died. I did not want them to die, but others, who call themselves Christians wanted vengeance in all its hatred and burnt the place. We were lucky that we did not die of exposure as we marched back to safety. Thank God, that I did not die of my wounds or the cold. No, my love, God cannot protect these fools. We need to go to the safety of Rhode Island."

"But what of my family, they will all be mad at you for taking me so far away," said Alice.

"They would be madder at me if you were dead and scalped, or taken prisoner like Mrs. Rowlandson," said Church. "There is no protecting that garrison until we learn to fight as well as the Indians do. Don't worry my dear, Plymouth will come calling for me soon enough, when they decide that they want to win this war. I will make short work of it."

"You are so sure of yourself Benjamin. How do you know that they will come calling?" asked Alice.

"I could be wrong," said Church. "I am not a papist; I am not the Pope speaking ex-cathedra," he stated in a false dramatic voice as she glared at him. "But if they don't call for me, and continue to fight and loose, Philip will drive them back to the sea, even Boston will be burnt and pillaged. We will be safe for now in Rhode Island. Hopefully, Mr. Williams will be able to maintain a good relationship with the Indians, but even Providence was attacked recently. We could always sail back to England, but then Massachusetts and Plymouth will have failed as colonies. No, they will call for me, and I will fight for them, on my terms."

"I like it better when you don't fight. Just stay on the island with me and we'll raise our family," said Alice.

"Raise our family, yes we will," said Church. "But when they call, I must answer."

"Two weeks after Church and his family arrived in the town of Portsmouth in Rhode Island, the Clark house, which was the garrison house in Plymouth was attacked by Totoson with eleven killed and many others wounded, the garrison house was burnt down," Temple Reported.

"More of the story later. Time for you boys to get some shut-eye." They leave, still stunned as if they had lost their best friend, or a major battle. Some shed a tear that night for their lost hero.

CHAPTER SEVEN

The War Drags On

THE KING PHILIP WAR—A RAID ON THE SETTLERS.

Commons.wikimedia.org

"Okay, boys, take a seat, quiet down and no horse play," says Temple as he organizes the barracks for the next story.

"Now, we'll talk about King Philips War without Church, Temple said.

"Yeah 'cause he deserted, that coward," said Peterson leaning on the post of one of the bunks in the hut.

"Yeah, like you did at Brandywine," replied Temple coldly.

"I didn't run, it was a retreat!" Peterson demanded.

"Yes, you ran and so did many others, forcing Brigader Preudhomme to call for a retreat. If you and yours had stood your ground, we might have won. Lucky for us General Greene was able to fill in," said Temple.

"You calling me a coward," said Peterson.

"Yes, I am!" replied Temple with a cold voice, tinged with hate. "And if you don't like it do something about it," he says as he throws down his jacket and rolls up his sleeves, getting ready to fight.

"I would, but I don't want to embarrass you in front of these boys," Peterson says as he slinks away and leaves the barracks.

Bridget, gives him a swift kick in the rear as he goes out the door.

"Bridget!" Temple exclaims. "My what aim you have. We should be as good with our muskets."

"Aye," she says in her thick Irish brough. "We women want you men coming back in one piece. Cowards like him make it dangerous for the whole lot of ya."

"Just like at Brandywine. How are you going to win a war with fools like that?" All the barracks breaks out in laughter. Toby hands him his jacket which he puts it back on. He brushes the dust off of his sleeves as he begins to tell the next part of the story.

"So, Peterson," Temple stumbles, "eh I mean Moseley is up to his old tricks again. If he can't find real enemies to fight, and usually loose to, he will make enemies out of peaceful Indians. This time he had some help from other Indian haters in Concord. They had written to Mosely and asked him to get rid of these Indians in their midst."

"John Hoar had been a friend of the Indians and a negotiator with them," Temple continued. "He had help to bring Mary Rowlandson back, along with Tom and Peter, two Praying Indians. In fact, when he first arrived at the scene to negotiate her release, Mary thought that they had shot him. She was in a wigwam, having been told that an Englishmen had come to the camp and she heard gun shots from multiple guns. She feared the worst, that the Englishman was dead, or badly wounded. It turns out that the Indians had shot above, below, in front of and behind his horse to intimidate him, and to show what they could do, if they wanted."

"Anyhow, Hoar was in charge of keeping a watch on the local Concord Praying Indians. He made sure that they had work to do during the day, and at night, they had their own barracks that they would report to keep the townsfolk safe, and to keep the Indians safe from the townsfolk."

"The townsfolk had animus for the Indians," Toby blurts out proudly.

"Quite right Toby, but what did I say about letting me tell the story?" said Temple as Jeremiah shoves him and the other boys throw debris his way.

"Sorry," Toby replied.

"And Moseley arrives in town on a Sunday, with his men and goes to the meeting house, said Temple. "He finds a small group of Indian haters such as himself. After conferring with them, he leads the group as a mob, goes down to where Hoar had his workhouse and demanded to inspect the Indians. He placed a guard at the door of the workhouse that night and in the morning, he had them come out. He then tied them all together with a rope around their necks, marched them to Boston where they were exiled to Deer Island."

"Boooo.." the boys jeer.

"So much for the brave Indian fighter," Smith says.

"Yes," Temple added, "this is the shameful part of the story. Deer Island was a place in Boston Harbor where many of the 'praying Indians' where sent, supposedly for their safety, but it was more like a prison sentence. Many would die there due to the harsh conditions, the cold of winter, and the lack of food. And Moseley and many others where more than glad to send any Indian there, Praying, friendly or enemy."

"Still other Indians are on the attack," said Temple. "Groton was one of the places attacked, which the Praying Indians, Tom and Peter, (who had been sent into the Indian villages as spies, risking their lives) had given information about. They also had given information about Lancaster and Marlboro, a couple of weeks before those places were attacked. All showing a lack of trust by the English for people whom they should have trusted, the 'Praying Indians.'"

"Now Longmeadow is just south of Springfield, on the Connecticut border and it is attacked," Temple continues. "Marlborough, the supply station for the Massachusetts army is attacked, the Nipmucks strike again near Sudbury, Rehoboth in Plymouth is attacked, and finally, March closes out with Providence RI being attacked."

"It was the day of March 26th that was one of the darkest days for the English in New England," Temple said. "On that Sunday at Longmeadow a group of the townspeople where heading to church services, not suspecting that they would come under attack. They were suddenly surrounded by Indians. Most were able to escape the ordeal, but a man and girl where killed. Also, two women, both holding a baby were seized and carried off. The militia group gave chase and caught the kidnappers, but not before the Indians killed the two babies and wounded both mothers."

"That same day a group of Indians were sneaking up on a meeting house in Marlborough when the people where there for service," recounted Temple. "The Pastor stepped out for a moment, it is said because of a tooth ache and spotted the Indians approaching. He warned the parishioners, but the attack was destructive. Many people abandoned Marlborough because of this attack, but it remained an important outpost because it was a supply depot for the Massachusetts army. Ephraim Curtis, of Brookfield fame, led a force of about 40 men and found the Indian camp where the attack was most likely launched from. They were able to chase them off and claimed that they had shot some of the Indians, but they couldn't determine the number of enemy casualties. That night the deserted town of Simsbury Connecticut was burnt."

"The worst disaster of the day happened along the Pawtucket River just a couple miles north of Providence," said Temple. "Captain Michael Pierce was in the Rehoboth area searching for Indians. He had received information that a group of Indians were camping by the river not far from where his troops were. He had 65 Englishmen plus 20 Indians. He also sent a messenger to Providence to ask for help. Then they set out on their mission. The messenger arrived at Providence in time for the Sunday worship and waited until it was over before making his announcement. Upon hearing it Captain Andrew Edmunds set out immediately with a militia to aid Pierce, but it was too late. Pierce's men came upon a huge group of Narragansetts who surrounded them. Pierce had his men firing in all directions, but they were overwhelmed. Those who survived and escaped were able to make it to Woodcock's garrison in Attleboro miles away, to tell their harrowing fate. Forty-two men were buried at the site. It was a dark day for the English."

"Roger Williams, whose home was in Providence couldn't save the town from being burnt, even though he among all the English was renowned for keeping on good terms with the Narragansetts, who attacked the town, said Temple. Even his house was burnt. Rumor has it that Williams grabbed his walking staff and at the age of 77 went out alone to meet the Narragansett sachem, Canonchet, who was leading the attack on Providence. Williams said:

> "'Massachusetts can raise thousands of men at this moment, and if you kill them, the King of England will supply their place as fast as they fall," Williams warned the chief.
>
> 'Well let them come, we are ready for them,' the chief replied. But as for you brother Williams, you are a good man; you have been kind to us many years; not a hair of your head shall be touched.'"[6]

"The success of the Indian attacks had caused the Massachusetts government to warn the people in the outlying areas to abandon their farms and homes and seek refuge in a safer and more easily defendable place," Temple said. "Some towns had already experienced this. Deerfield, Northfield, and Brookfield had already been abandoned. Now, the colonial authorities were telling other communities like Hatfield and Northampton to abandon their towns and head for Hadley and for those in Westfield to go into Springfield. Many of the people

---

[6] Eric B. Schultz, Michael J. Tougas, King Philips War (New York: Countryman Press, 1999) 283

refused to leave their farms and lands that they had worked so hard for and stayed put. Now, whether they would get military assistance of Boston after having refused to leave is another question. The three towns of Hatfield, Northampton and Hadley formed a tight nucleus that could render aid to each other when needed. This is exactly what happened with the Battle of Bloody Brook. Both Captain Moseley in the field nearby and Major Treat at Hadley came to the aid of the people leaving Deerfield, being led by Captain Lathrop. It was a bloody, expensive battle, 64 Englishmen died, and untold Indians. But the towns were able to defend themselves, with the aid of troops from Massachusetts and Connecticut. So, when the people of those town were told to abandon their lands by the Magistrates in faraway Boston, they said, 'No, just give us some men and we can defend ourselves.' This brings in the other problem, people in more defensible or more populous areas, like Boston, started to refuse to answer the call to arms for those who would not abandon their farms. They dodged the draft or didn't show up for ordered mustering. They did not want to die defending someone else's farm. Also, the people of Westfield, if they were forced to abandon their lands would retreat to Connecticut, not Springfield, thus their loyalties were to Hartford, not Boston. The United Colonies were not so united."

"This was a short one tonight, tomorrow we talk about Sudbury. It is pivotable," Said Temple.

"Tell us now" Toby begs.

"No. You all need some sleep. I hear Von Steuben has something special for us tomorrow," said Temple.

"Aahhh," the boys lament and grumble on their way out.

CHAPTER EIGHT

The Town of Sudbury

Brentbooks.blogspot.com

"Okay boys find a seat and settle down. This one will be interesting," Temple starts. The boys grab their spots look up to him in rapt attention.

"I'm going to tell you about the sad fate of the town of Sudbury Massachusetts, but it is a day that will change the war, though it wasn't really obvious to many at the time," said Temple. "So, we'll start with Mary Rowlandson first."

"Why her?" Toby complains.

"Hush-up boy and listen," Temple says. "Parts of her book give a real insight to what was going on in the Indian village. We have plenty of writings by the English, hers is a window few English had. She was in the Indian wigwam, their meeting room/living quarters/dinner hall, they came in various sizes and are used for many purposes. This was one where they held a war dance."

"They let her in on their war dance!" Toby exclaims incredibly.

"Yes, they did," said Temple. "They had nothing to fear from her, so they allowed her in. In her book she writes about the war dance, and she starts it off by speaking about a 'Praying Indian.' She wrote:

> "'Another Praying-Indian, went to the Sudbury fight, and his squaw also with him with her papoos on her back. Before they went to that fight, they got a company together to powwow; the manner was as followeth. There was one that kneeled on a Deer-skin, with the company around him in a ring who kneeled and striking upon the ground with their hands, and with sticks, and muttering or humming with their mouths, besides him who kneeled in the ring, there also stood one with a Gun in his hand: Then he on the deer-skin made a speech, and all manifested assent to it and so they did many times together. Then they bade him with the Gun go out of the ring, which he did, but when he was out, they called him in again; but he seemed to make a stand, then they called the more earnestly, till he returned again: Then they all sang. Then they gave him two guns, in either hand one: And so he on the deer-skin began again; and at the end of every sentence in his speaking, they all assented, humming or muttering with their mouths, and striking upon the ground with their hands. Then bade they him with the two Guns go out of the ring again; which he did a little way. Then they call him in again, but he made a stand; so they called him with greater earnest; but he stood reeling and wavering as if he knew not whither he should stand or fall, or which way to go. Then they called him with exceeding great vehemency, all of them one and

another: after a little while he turned in, staggering as he went, with his arms stretched out, in either hand a Gun. As soon as he came in, they all sang and rejoiced exceedingly a while. And then he upon the Deer-skin, made another speech unto which they all assented in a rejoicing manner: and so they ended their business and forthwith went to Sudbury-fight. To my thinking they went without any scruple, but that they should prosper, and gain the victory."[7]

"With that they went out to attack Sudbury," said Temple. "The town had become very isolated of late. Groton, Lancaster Mendon had all been abandoned. Marlborough might have as well, except that it was the supply depot for the Connecticut River Valley towns. The army didn't want to abandon that, but it was depleted of its populous. Those are all in an arch around Sudbury. The Indians probably wouldn't want to attack Marlborough because that would be too heavily defended. That left Sudbury as the lone outpost of English towns that was ripe for an attack. As you can see with Mrs. Rowlandson's account, Sudbury was the next target. What is odd is that on the evening of April 20th Captain Samuel Wadsworth had marched 70 men on the Marlboro Road through Sudbury to Marlborough to reinforce the garrison there. They were sent out of Boston by the Colonial Council of War because they had received information that a large group of Indians had been gathering at Wachusett Mountain. What they didn't know was that 500 Indians, possibly including Philip where already gaining their position in and around Sudbury as the small force marched through. They arrived at Marlborough, hardly had time to recover from the march, when first thing in the morning they get the news that Sudbury was under attack, and they would have to march right back there. They also had the troops from Marlborough under Captain Samuel Brocklebank."

---

[7] The Sovereignty and Goodness of God by Mary Rowlandson with related documents edited by Neal Salisbury page 100

"Most of the people in Sudbury were already in garrison houses because of the precarious, dangerous position that they all knew that they were in," said Temple. "In fact, some of the garrison houses would brick up the inside of a house, especially in the sleeping areas to protect the people inside from being shot by the Indians. The Indians would take pot shots at the garrison house, and there were bands of Nipmucks and Wampanoags around the house, attacking it, there were plenty of other Indians going around, plundering the other houses and farms, and burning the structures once they had stolen what they wanted out of it."

"All the surrounding towns knew of the battle in a short amount of time, and there was no shortage of attempts by the English to defend Sudbury," said Temple. "Concord sent out a dozen or so, brave, but foolish men who were quickly devoured by the Indian juggernaut once they arrived there. One of them may even have been captured and held for a later fate of torture. Another group from Watertown did much better. They arrived safely and joined with the townsmen and helped to push the Indians to the western side of the Sudbury River. While this was going on Captains Wadsworth and Brocklebank arrived on the scene on the other side of Sudbury. They saw a small party of Indians who immediately retreated from them. They followed this small group, thinking that they could handle them, when once again, a part of the English army fell right inside of a trap. They were surrounded by Indians. They were able however to fight their way to the top of a nearby hill, Green Hill, that gave them somewhat of an advantage. The Watertown men heard the fighting at the other end of the town and ran to Wadsworth's defense on Green Hill but were eventually driven back by the Indian forces. By midday news of the fight had even reached Charlestown, at least 20 miles away, next to Boston and they had troops ride out on horse and a group of Praying Indians on foot who raced to the scene. Obviously, the horsemen, led by Corporal Solomon Phipps got there first, in time to engage in the fight. There were also troopers riding in from Brookfield going to Boston who got drawn into the battle. After losing four of his 18 men, Captain Edward Cowell was able to unite with Phipps late in the day. And another military group came from Marlborough under Captain John Cutler and almost fell into another trap but managed to avoid it. Late in the afternoon, the battle was reaching a pivotal moment. The Indians set fire to the dry brush on Green Hill. The smoke and fire drove Wadsworth's troops into abandoning the high point in terror. The Indians were able to fire upon them at will as the Englishmen fled the flames. Wadsworth's force lost about 30 men including Wadsworth and Brocklebank. Some 15 or so made it to the safety of a reinforced mill, the Indians, having gotten their victory faded away into the forest."

"The Praying Indians who came from Charlestown arrived once the battle was over," said Temple. "But they still provided a good service by searching the woods and confirming that the Nipmucks had left the area. They also helped to bury the dead soldiers, which proved to be a well needed comfort to the English and went a long way to healing the divide between the Praying Indians and some of the more hateful English."

"It was a destructive day for the English," Temple said. "But the Indians were subdued about their victory, at least according to Mrs. Rowlandson' account. In the past the Indians had come back into the village rejoicing in their exploits, chanting out their great deeds and counting off the number of dead Englishmen long before they entered the village. Mrs. Rowlandson said that the returning warriors were oddly quiet." Rowlandson wrote;

> "They said that they had killed two captains, and almost 100 men. One Englishman they brought along with them said that it was too true, for they had made sad work at Sudbury, as it indeed proved. Yet they came home without that rejoicing and triumphing over their victory which they were wont to shew at other times, but rather like Dogs (as they say) which have lost their ears. Yet I could not perceive that it was for their own loss of men: they said that they have not lost above five or six: and I missed none, except in one Wigwam. When they went, they acted as if the Devil had told them that they should win a great victory: and now

they acted, as if the Devil had told them they should have a fall."[8]

"It was a devastating defeat for the English," said Temple. "They had lost many men. And they were still making the same mistakes that they had been making at the beginning of the war. The English were still blindly walking into ambushes."

"Mr. Church wouldn't do that" Toby blurts out.

"Quite right, but don't get ahead of me," Temple said. "There is still a lot of fighting to go. At Sudbury, it was still the English who were holding the ground. And they had shown that they could rally to a fight when they had to. There was something missing. And that missing element was learning how to fight like an Indian. The English were still exposing themselves and setting themselves up for defeat. Ever so slowly they would realize that they needed the help of the Praying Indians to fight the "heathen Indians," as Mrs. Rowlandson would say. In the meantime, some Englishmen were still on a suicide mission and the Indians were more than happy to help them hang themselves."

"Sudbury was a great victory for the Indians, but it was their last one in the western part of Massachusetts, and for that matter the rest of the war," Temple said. "But it was not yet obvious. One of the big problems that both sides had was their need to grow food. The war took the fields for growing away from both sides, but the Indians felt it greater than the English did. The Wampanoags and the Narragansetts had been driven off their lands. The Nipmucks where still in their own territory, but the war waged and armies marched throughout their lands destroying crops and preventing normal planting from taking place. The English still controlled a greater expanse of the land and though the Indians had done great damage to their outlying farms, and even raided Plymouth and Weymouth at times, the English could still depend on crops from elsewhere. Connecticut, though it was heavily involved with the war, saw little action on its home territory. Not so the Indians. One of the accomplishments of the Great Swamp battle was that it took away the

---

[8] Ibid 101

Narragansett's winter storage and their seed for the following spring. The Indians became dependent upon foraging, as we saw with Mrs. Rowlandson, and stealing crops or cattle from the English. Of course, this would be the immediate cause of the next battle."

"The Nipmucks are in the western Massachusetts- Connecticut River Valley area," said Temple. "Their raid on Sudbury had been highly successful, but they were in desperate need of food. So, they went to one of their favorite fishing areas, Peskeompscut about five miles north of Deerfield on the Connecticut River. In fact, the name of the river in the Indian would be Kwinitekw which the English interpreted to the Connecticut River. The Indian name means "Long River, so the English actually are calling it the Long River River. It starts up near Canada. Anyhow, there was a falls at Peskeompscut which was rich with fish runs of the Atlantic Salmon as they came in from the ocean to spawn in their home birthplace. It was also full with other fish as well, like trout that were there year-round. So, the hungry Indians had plenty to choose from there. And they had raided the town of Hatfield and had made off with a large number of cattle and sheep. It was a time of feasting for the Nipmucks, Narragansetts and the Wampanoags."

"On May 13th one of the captives that the Indians were holding, Thomas Reed, a soldier taken in a previous raid, escaped and made his way to Hadley and told the people there of the encampment at Peskeompscut," Temple said. "He said that it was a large camp, but few warriors. Also, he claimed that they had let down their guard thinking that they were in a safe place. Captain William Turner listened with great interest. Though he himself was ill, this could be an opportunity for retaliation for Sudbury, the last attack, and all the other attacks and depredations that the English had had to endure over the past 10 months of this war. The problem was that there was no organized military at the garrison at that time, just the townsfolk of the three towns of Hadley, Hatfield, and Northampton. Turner sent word down to Hartford to send reinforcements, but the message was that they would not come immediately. The men of the towns declared that they were ready to ride into battle, Turner had a force of 150-160 inexperienced, but eager soldiers; men, boys, and servants to do battle with the Indians. So, they rode out on May 18th. As they rode north, they had to pass over the tragic site of Bloody Brook and through the burnt-out Deerfield village. Possibly they had the images of the murderous attacks on their fellow citizens, brothers, fathers, mothers, and sisters running through their heads to fuel their lust for vengeance. They came to within a half a mile of the encampment, dismounted, tied their horses to the trees, leaving a couple men to guard them and then set off through the woods to find their enemy. As we talked about before, the English were not good at stealth approaches, like the Indians were. But they were aided by a rain that was muffling their approach, as well as the roaring rapids of the falls which would have been full due to spring runoff. Silently they crept into the Indian village, until they each positioned themselves in front of a wigwam. Then all of a sudden, they fired into the opening of the enclosures, ensuring that the inhabitants could not easily escape and so tore through the encampment. Those that were able to scurry out, whether it was between reloading attempts by the English, or they managed to break out some other way, fled into the rapids of the river. Some were clinging to the rocks, others tried to hide in the cut out of the bank, some were swept away and drowned downriver. The English made good and sure that they killed as many Indians as they could no matter where they were, what age or gender. It was a slaughter of massive numbers. Then they went back to the camp to plunder it and see what they could find. There were two blacksmith forges which were used to repair the Indians guns and pigs of lead to make musket balls, these were thrown in the river. Then they found another captive who told them that there were a lot more Indians around and that they should get out as soon as possible."

"Captain Turner realized this same thing, almost too late," said Temple. "He sounded retreat and the English hightailed it out of there just as the other Indians from nearby camps were beginning to come down to aide their brethren in the battle. The English barely made it to their horses before their retreat was cut off, but not before Captain Turner was shot in the leg. He soon fell off his horse and died were he fell. His second in Command led the men through the retreat and was able to prevent a massacre of the English. Not all the men were able to get back on their mounts. Before the Indians had retaliated, the English had lost only one man, and that was by being shot by another Englishman, who mistook him for an Indian as he exited a wigwam. But in the retreat, which actually had turned into a rout an additional 37 Englishmen were killed. They had stayed there too long, their inexperience got them killed. But they had done very great damage to the Indians having killed as it was reported somewhere between 100 to 200 Indians. The English were not safe until they had made it to Deerfield. Then they made the slow ride home to Hadley."

"Hartford got news of the action, realized that it was a serious situation and sent 80 men under Captain Benjamin Newbury to strengthen the upper valley," said Temple. "It was not a case of too little too late. Because the Indians would attack Hatfield in retribution for the attack at the Falls, but with fresh troops, the Indian attack was rebuffed."

"Now there was a flurry of activity by the English for a new intercolonial expedition," said Temple. "Massachusetts sent out 500 men, and Connecticut sent out an additional force, led by Major Talcott, of 440 Englishmen and Indians. The idea for the Massachusetts men was to root out the Indians in the Mount Wachusett area and then rendezvous with the Connecticut forces. On his march north Talcott found an abandoned Indian village, then had a skirmish with a small force where the English killed or captured 52 warriors. Talcott then proceeded to Quaboag which was about halfway between Springfield and Marlborough. He was impatient for the arrival of the Massachusetts troops under the command of Major Daniel Henchmen. In an unprofessional dig at Henchman, he sent an unsealed message to the other leader, intending for everyone it passed through to read him complaining about Henchman's tardiness. Then Talcott marched to Hadley where he joined forces with Newbury to create a force of 500 men. Unbeknownst… that's another big preacher word meaning that Henchman was doing his job well as he tried to unite with Talcott," the boys laughed.

"Unbeknownst to Talcott, Henchman had headed to Wachusett, surprised a group of Indians fishing in a pond near Lancaster, killed seven and captured 29," said Temple. "Then he headed back down to

Marlborough, reloaded with ammunition and headed out to meet-up with Talcott. While Talcott was waiting an Indian force attacked Hadley, and they were able to easily beat them away. Afterwards it was reported that a band of Mohawks had attacked the Indian village, while the men were attacking Hadley. Many of their women and children were killed and possessions lost."

"The month of June was looking awfully bad for the Indians," said Temple. "It seems like the English might be able to turn the tide of the war and it also seems like there was a parting of the way between the Nipmucks and Philip. Some of the Indians might now be blaming their bad luck on the man responsible for starting the war."

"Henchman finally united with Talcott and they proceeded to search for the enemy up the river," said Temple. "The Massachusetts forces on one side, the Connecticut boys on the other. They made it as far as Squakeag up near the Vermont/New Hampshire border, but the Indians were long gone. It was disappointing to have such a large force, and nothing to do but march in the wet weather. Talcott and his troops went back to Hartford, with the understanding that they would return. They never did. Henchman realizing that there was no need for so many troops to be idle there, left enough to strengthen the garrisons and headed back east. He left a garrison in Quinsigamond, now Worcester, with orders to keep an eye on the Wachusett, Lancaster area, and then proceeded on to Marlborough."

"Things were beginning to heat up in the Plymouth Colony again," according to Temple. "Early in May four Englishmen were killed in Taunton, there were several raids, including one in Bridgewater. Indians were being spotted everywhere from Cohasset to Taunton to Assawompsett Pond to Dartmouth. Captain Brattle came upon a group of them fishing in the Pawtucket River, killing a number of them, and spoiling their catch."

"Early in June the government of Plymouth was planning to organize a force of about 150 English and fifty Indians to patrol the Colony," Temple says with a smile and emphasizing the next couple of words to reintroduce Church. "And who do you think shows-up, out of the blue."

"Captain Benjamin," Toby and Jeremiah jump up and shout. "Yeaaah! Hip, hip Hooray," "Hip, hip Hooray," all the boys shout.

"That's right, Captain Benjamin," says Temple with a smirk. "And that's where we pick up the story tomorrow. Captain Benjamin is back in the fight, and he has what he wants. A mixed band of Englishmen and Indians. He is ready to do battle. But that tomorrow night's story. That is all for now."

"No, we have to hear about Captain Benjamin, we won't be able to sleep," complains Toby to no avail.

"That's all for now boy's, tomorrow night," Temple says. "Get going," he orders.

CHAPTER NINE

Captain Benjamin is Back

Indians fishing by the river. Pinterest.com

"Mister. Temple, Mister Temple," Toby shouts as he bursts into the barracks.

"Mister Peterson hasn't been at roll-call for two days now," Toby says breathlessly with Jeremiah coming in behind him. "Some people are saying that he has deserted."

"Good, we're better off without him," Temple replies coldly. "We don't need cowards like him in the line. We need men we can depend on. If you don't carry out your job, if you cut and run you endanger every man in the line. I don't care what your job is. Cannoneer, infantry, drummer-boy," he says as he looks around the room. Then looking at the boys he asks, "Can we depend on you boys?"

"Yes sir," they all say jumping to their feet and saluting.

"Good, that's good, I knew I could count on you all. We better not ever find Peterson," Temple says. "It will not go well for him. Take a seat boys, take a seat and get warm. We are getting to the meat of the story now;" Temple says, as more boys then ever boys fill the tiny barracks where he does his story telling. The men in the barracks have grudgingly accepted this nightly invasion, because deep within, they love the story too.

"So, after the English successes at Deerfield, it has seemed that the tide had certainly shifted toward the English," said Temple. "Many Indians were giving up in the field or surrendering to the English before they were caught in battle. Their thinking was that if they gave themselves up willingly, rather than be caught in battle, that they would fare better, not get executed or sold into slavery. Some came in cursing Philip, or others who led them into the battle. One such large surrender in Boston was a group of Nipmucks, 180 strong who gave up the fight. Sagamore John, one of their prominent men brought the group into the English town and presented alive his former proud chieftain, led with a rope around his neck, Matoonas. He was notorious for some of the first attacks on the Massachusetts Bay Colony, such as Mendon, and was high on any kill or capture list in the English army. It was obvious Philip was no longer welcome among the Nipmucks and he might have even feared for his life, or that he would be marched into Boston as a peace offering to the English as Matoonas was. He would flee back into his home territory of Plymouth were the war had started from in the first place. Why he didn't run up north into Canada and into the arms of the French, I don't know. Maybe he wanted to make one last desperate stand. Kill or be killed. Drive Plymouth into the sea or be hunted down like a rabid dog. We will never know. But now the war goes back to where it started from, Church's territory. As for Matoonas, the English made short work of him. When the Nipmucks marched him into town they didn't even bother with a trial, it was just summary execution. He was brought into the Boston Commons, tied to a tree, and the English ordered him to be shot by Sagamore John and his men. I guess that proved to the English just how serious the surrendering Nipmucks were for peace."

"But Philip is as elusive as ever even though there are more men in the field hunting him down," said Temple.

"Finally, Church gets his approval for his command," Temple reported. "Just as the Magistrates where thinking about organizing a mixed-race command, the man who had first raised the idea four months prior walked into the assembly hall. He had not been able to eat or sleep well during his time away and no longer waited for them to come knocking. But still it was as if Providence was guiding him, because now the magistrates would listen to what he had to say. (He would still need further approval from the governor though.) Even Moseley had gotten tired of walking his men into ambushes and realized that he at least needed Indian scouts to warn him of waiting traps. The first thing that Church does is to return to Aquidneck Island by boat going around Cape Cod, but for some reason it leaves him off in the Elizabeth Islands in Buzzards Bay. So, he needs to hire out two 'friend Indians' of the Sakonnet tribe to canoe him the rest of the way to Aquidneck Island, about a 35-mile canoe trip. About three quarters of the way there, they come to Sakonnet point, a jut of land protruding out into the Rhode Island Sound. There a small group of Indians were fishing off of the rocky outcrop and Church had his pilots paddle him closer to shore so that he could speak to them. He had to yell to be heard over the water lapping on the shore, but they seemed to recognize each other. Both groups where suspicious of each other. Church told the Indians that his pilots were of the same tribe. The Indians spoke in their native language and they agreed to go to shore and talk face to face. When Church did, they immediately recognized each other. One of the Sakonnets was Honest George, the Indian who almost a year ago now had invited Church to the Sakonnet meeting where Church spoke to the female sachem Awashonks who at that time spoke of possibly having peace with the English. That is why Church took this risky move, to come to shore, he had never believed that Awashonks wanted war with the English then, and he believed that he could hammer out a peace deal between the two peoples now. So, he is talking with Honest George and he sets-up conference with Awashonks, her son Petonwowet, (Peter Nunnuit to the English), their chief captain, Nompash, and of course Honest George. They determined that he would return in two days, weather permitting. He had to be able to canoe the several miles from Aquidneck Island to the Sakonnet Point."

"So, he heads home and tells his wife all his plans," said Temple. "Alice, thinks that he is crazy, that she'll never see him again because the Indians will kill him. She is afraid that she will become a widow and her two young sons, one only three months old would be fatherless. He reassured her that they all were in God's protective hands and leaves her temporarily. He then goes to the colonial authorities in Newport to get their permission to confer with the Sakonnets. They refuse to give him any authority from the Colony and are as convinced as his wife that he is mad and a dead man if he returns to go to the meeting. But they do not stop him from what they think is a foolhardy and suicidal attempt. Before he leaves Newport, he gets some rum and tobacco, negotiating tools for the conference."

"Church goes back home to his wife, leaves her again, 'now almost broken hearted,' he wrote in his book, takes one of his servants with him, meets with the Indian canoe 'pilots' and heads to the rendezvous at Sakonnet Point at what is now called 'Treaty Rock,'" said Temple. "They arrive in two boats. Honest George is on the shore and greets him, pulling the canoe onto the beach. The other canoe stayed out in the deeper water just in case things went wrong and the Newport authorities and Alice Church were proven right. Church goes ashore and meets with Awashonks, Perter Nunnuit, and Nompash, and all looks good until they walk over to the Rock to discuss things. There the whole tribe was waiting in the tall grass for Church to come on over. They were dressed for warfare. Their bodies where slick, their hair in war mode, faces painted with war paint, guns and clubs in their hands. Church was a little bit surprised at the cold reception, but he did not flinch when they came out of the grass and surrounded them. After all, John Hoar went to negotiate for Mrs. Rowlandson's release he was met with a negotiating team that shot above him, under his horse, in front and in back of him. It seems like the Indians had their own negotiating habit of trying to thoroughly intimidate the other negotiator before things even got started. He calmly stated that George:

> 'had informed him that Awashonks had a desire to see him, and discourse about making peace with the English. She answered yes. Then said Mr. Church, 'It is customary when People meet to treat of Peace to lay aside their Arms, and to not appear in such Hostile form as your People do.'[9]

"When the Indians understood what he was saying, (some of them spoke English), there was quite a murmuring among them," Temple said. "Awashonks asked him which arms they should lay down and he stated, the guns, that they should put them a 'little way away.' This still left them with their war clubs but having looked at the crowd of warlike Indians and weighing his options, he only asked them to put their guns aside."

"Church was not out of hot water yet," said Temple. "He offered Awashonks some of his rum and asked her if she had forgotten about drinking 'occapechees,' a shot of strong drink. He raised his Callebash, a drinking vessel made out of a dried gourd, and slugged it down. She watched to see if he swallowed it or was faking it. He offered her the shell, but she insisted that he drink from it again. First, he poured some into his hand and drank it. He then reassured her that there was no poison in it, poured some more rum in the gourd and drank again. So according to his book, Church says that to prove its safety he passed the bottle to a "little ill looking fellow" and just as he was about to drink it straight from the bottle, church grabs him by the throat and takes the bottle away from him. "Do you intend to drink it shell and all?" he questions the man. Then gave it to Awashonks who took a hearty swig and passed it on to her attendants. He then pulled out his tobacco, spread it around and then they began to negotiate."

---

[9] The History of King Philips War By Benjamin Church Forgotten Books 2015 page 80

"Awashonks claimed that she was a little put off by him because he did not keep his previous promise of a year ago to return to her and tell her if the English were going to go to war or not," said Temple. "He told her that war broke out so suddenly when he was in Plymouth and he was called to become a soldier, that he couldn't return to speak to her. He told her that this was the first time that he could come here with any sort of authority to speak about Plymouth. She claimed that if he had returned with some solid promise from Plymouth, they might not have joined with Philip in the first place. Then Church said that he had wanted to come and speak to her and that he was in the Punkateese area with 19 of his men when they did battle with some Indians, (it was these Sakonnets who had surrounded him at the Pease Field Battle) and that they fought for the better part of the afternoon. Suddenly there was a noise and much loud murmuring and arguing. One of the Sakonnets raised his tomahawk over his head and would have run at Church but was held back by others as he yelled at Church in his language. The interpreter asked Church if he knew what the warrior had said, Church replied "No." The interpreter says that he claims that you killed his brother and now he "thirsts for your blood." Church stated that "his brother began first" that he was looking for Indians to speak to and they fired first."

"Then Nompash, the chief warrior, commanded silence and told the Indians that they should not talk about old things now. The situation calmed down and the parties were able to get back to talking about arranging a peace deal with the English. Church asked what Awashonks wanted him to tell the English in order that they would break away from Philip. He reminded them, that he was not there as an emissary of the governor, but, if the requests were reasonable, "the Government would not be unreasonable, and that he would use his interest in the Government for them." He reminded them that the Pequots were once enemies with the English and that they now had a good relationship with them. He assured them that he would be able to convince the government in Plymouth;

> 'That they (the Sakonnets) and all them...should have their lives spared and none transported out of the country, (if) they would subject themselves to them (Plymouth), and serve them in what they were able.'[10]

"He again reassured them that Plymouth would not try to move them out of their home country and how pleased "he was with the thoughts of their return, and of the former friendship that had been between them, & c."[11]

> Nompash rose up 'and expressed the great value and respect he had for Mr. Church; and bowing to him said, Sir, if you please to accept of me and my men, and will head us, we'll fight for you, and will help you to Philip's head before Indian corn be ripe.'[12]

"With that the peace talks where concluded, Church could visit his lovely Alice again to show her he was alive and well, before going to Plymouth to promise the surrender of the Sakonnets. Peter Nunnuit went ahead of Church to Plymouth to confer with the magistrates," said Temple.

"Soon thereafter Church rejoins Major William Bradford who had showed up in Pocasset, a few miles north of the Sakonnets, with the new Command of Plymouth forces," said Temple. "Church's commission had not yet been approved by the Governor, so he was still marching with Bradford. Church informed Awashonks that Bradford had come and was apprised, told, about the deal that they struck. Bradford would not release the warriors to Church at this time, but instead, when Bradford met with Awashonks and he instructed them to go to Sandwich, about 10 to 15 miles south of Plymouth to wait for further instructions. So, they walked there under a flag of truce, nobody bothered them. Bradford's troops got into a boat to take them across the Sakonnet

---

[10] Ibid 84
[11] Ibid 84
[12] Ibid 84

River into Mount Hope Bay, when they spotted fires, most likely from Indians on the shore of the Mount Hope peninsula. Church, assuming it was Philip's people, (the English had been given information that they were clamming in the area) wanted to head straight towards the fires. But Bradford had the ships go to the tip of the peninsula to encircle and trap the wily Philip. Again, it was a failed plan. But the force was strengthened by the arrival of Captain Brattle and his eighty men, as well as a later arrival of Captain Moseley and his crew."

"About this time the English were rolling up huge victories in Narragansett country," said Temple. "In early June, Major Talcott, fresh off his northern patrol up the Connecticut River, was in northwestern Rhode Island now. Marching through the Nipsachuck area they captured four Indians who gave them information about the movements of Philip. Talcott and his troops, 300 Englishmen and 100 Indians, continued to search for the illusive fugitive and came upon a large group of Narragansetts. Talcott engaged them in battle, and they ran towards a swamp to hide there. But the English were no longer afraid of swamp fighting and the Indians may have been low on ammunition anyhow. Also, the English horsemen had surrounded the swamp with the Indians leading the advance into the swamp. On top of that there was a drought this year, so the swamp was dry and the vegetation not as lush as the previous year. All that added up to good luck for the English. Talcott's crew killed or captured 171 Narragansett that day including men women and children. The Pequots and the Mohegans took 45 prisoners, being women and children. Found among the dead was saunk squaw (the old queen) Quaiapin, Ningret's sister. (Ningret was a Sachem of the Niantick tribe which had always been friendly to the English.)"

"After this raid Talcott marched down to Warwick," said Temple. "He found there a group of 80 Narragansett who were waiting there for their leader, Potuck to return from Newport with possible terms for peace. Talcott was not looking for peace, but rather engaged the Narragansetts in battle. They killed or captured 67 that day. About this time Bradford had sent a message to Talcott asking him to come join the expedition to hunt down Philip. Talcott wanted to, but his

Indians said that they had to bring their captives and other plunder home. He dared not proceed without his Indians, so Talcott declined to join the expedition. Also, the Massachusetts authorities had sent a peace envoy to the Narragansetts, Peter Ephraim by name. He had gotten captured by the Connecticut troops. At first Connecticut was mad that Massachusetts would try to sue for a separate peace, but it wasn't a big enough schism to endanger the United Colonies. Rather, it was indicative of the divisions now beginning to show in the Indian alliance which had never been more than an opportunity to be sized upon by many of the tribes. Now that the opportunities were no longer there, many of the Indians wanted out of the fight. Not so Philip. The war started with him; it would finish with him."

"Not everything was going well for the English at the beginning of the summer 1676," said Temple. "During the heat of the battle, when the English are turning the tide of the war, a special Agent of the Crown Edward Randolph shows up in Boston. He was largely unimpressed with the war effort, but he was here to see if the colony was measuring up to the Crown's rules and regulations regarding the imperial system. So, in the middle of a life-or-death struggle for the Colonies, Massachusetts had to deal with a know-nothing blowhard whose reports back to the king were completely erroneous. He gave all the success of the war to Plymouth Colony, downplaying both the efforts by Massachusetts and Connecticut."

"Anyhow, on July 6th, a black servant, Jethro, who had been taken prisoner at Swansea a week earlier, was rescued," said Temple. "He had important information about an impending attack. He had a good working knowledge of the Wampanoag language and he overheard their plans to attack Taunton. So, Bradford reinforced the town with soldiers and when the Wampanoags did attack, they were quickly rebuffed. What is curious is that Taunton's force had been depleted five days prior to the attack. So, the information was doubly important. Without the reinforcement, the town could have been devastated. But the Taunton force out on patrol did good work as well. They came upon a group of Indians and captured about 20 to 30 of them. They also captured an old Indian who told them that he would lead them to Philip, but he had left the camp. The trail was cold because he had left earlier in the day."

"The English troops kept searching for Philip. Again, they encountered a large group of Indians, killed, or captured a good amount, but the majority fled away into the woods. Philip was nowhere to be found. By July 16th, the troops returned to Taunton to regroup and plan," said Temple.

"During this time, Church had reported to the governor at Plymouth about the course of the war," said Temple. "While there, the governor informed him that he had accepted the peace terms that Church had made with Awashonks. That meant that Church was now free to gather together his warriors and the Englishmen who would volunteer to march with him and go hunt down Philip."

"Hip hip, hooray. Hip, hip hooray. Hip hip, hooray" all the boys yell out.

"That's right," Temple said. "Now we're getting somewhere. But he still has to gather all of his men. So, he took a few Englishmen with him and went over to Sandwich to find the Sakonnets. But they weren't there. They searched for them and found the Sakonnets in Buzzards Bay near the Sippican and Weweantic Rivers. They were having a feast on the beach with horse races, wrestling matches, other sports, and dances. Church makes contact with one of them, not wanting to spook a shooting due to mistaken identity and he was invited in to dine with them. They had eel, flatfish, bass, and shellfish; a feast fit for a king. After eating the Sakonnets held a war dance, probably much like the one that Mrs. Rowlandson had witnessed. They had a ring of people in front of a fire. Warriors would go between the ring and the fire, dancing around it with a spear in one hand and a hatchet in the other as they did battle with the fire all the time naming out tribes and people with whom they had done battle. When one warrior ended his dance another would start up, all trying to out fight the previous warrior. Finally, Nompash, Captain of the guard came to Church and said:

'They were making soldiers for him, and what they had been doing was all of them Swearing of them and having that in manner engaged all the lusty stout men.'[13]

"Awashonks assured him that all the men were ready to go into battle with him, and all he had to do was to pick those whom he wanted," said Temple. "There is some question to the exact date that Church and his men set out into the woods to hunt for Philip, but it probably was about the 10th to the 14th of July 1676. This is important because things will happen fast and furious from here on out. More about the exploits of Captain Church tomorrow night boys."

"Nooo, just when it was getting good. We want more about Captain Church," the boys lamented.

"Quit complaining, there's plenty left. Go get some shut-eye now," says Temple as the boys get up and shuffle out, slightly disappointed, but already anticipating the next night's story.

---

[13] Ibid 100

CHAPTER TEN

The Hunt is On

King Philip lies dead after being shot. Commons.wikimedia.org

A gain, the small hut is packed. Even the crusty, cynical men have been enjoying this intrusion on their limited privacy. Temple gets up front and begins.

"Church quickly made a reputation for himself and his mixed-race army," Temple says. "He seems to have totally thrown away the English rule book of fighting protocols and took on the Indian way like as if he had been born into it. The Indians made the best scouts, so his Sakonnets would lead the way through the woods. When they saw a group of the enemy, they would report back to Church who would attempt if possible, to surround the enemy camp so that no one could escape. Now, you have to realize that these men fought as mercenaries of sorts. Plymouth was to provision them, and in return, the government got half of the captives and arms that they captured. The English Captains and men got the other half of the captives and arms, and the Indians got to plunder the rest. Church thought that this was 'poor incouragement' for his soldiers, but the pay was later increased. The captives, if they were leaders of the war, they were to be executed, the rest usually sold into slavery. Some became slaves to local people where they would have shorter sentences and could be released at the end of a term. Others were packed away on slave ships to be sold into slavery in the Caribbean, if they would have them, and some to Africa. The Indians made very rebellious slaves and so some places would not take them at all. But that was someone else's concern, the men fighting the battle were getting their pay, their 'incouragement' as Church called it. Church repeated these actions time and time again, so much so that the Magistrates expanded Church's commission, and approved of him taking on more men."

> "The Government observing his extraordinary courage and conduct, and the successes from Heaven added to it saw cause to inlarge his Commission; gave him the power to raise and dismiss his forces, as he should see occasion; to 'Commissionate Officers under him, and should march as far as he should see cause, within the limits of the three United Colonies: to receive mercy, give quarter, or not; excepting some particular & noted Murderers: viz Philip and all that were at the destroying of Mr. Clark's Garrison, and some few others.'"[14]

---

[14] Ibid 104

"There is a curious thing about Captain Church," said Temple. "He is a great commander, but does not take well to be commanded, especially when he sees an advantage or an opportunity to attack the enemy. I am not saying that he was insubordinate, but he chaffed greatly when compelled to do a duty that was not involved with conducting open warfare. He hated the idea of building forts instead of chasing the enemy through the woods. He turned down a command post in the Great Swamp Fight, then realized that he needed to be in the fight, not directing it from outside of it. Now he was put on a duty to guard provisions that were being sent from Plymouth to Major Bradford in Taunton. He knew that it was an important thing to provision the army, it is just that it didn't fit him well. So, he found someone else who would guard it as far as Middleborough, from there he would have to take charge to bring it to Taunton. But he stayed around the carts, hoping to attract the enemy, being free from the guard duty, he could spring a trap on them. This plan worked fairly well, and Church was able to capture 16 enemy Indians. These captives also informed him that Tispaquin, 'The Black Sachem,' was at Assawompsett, not far from Taunton. But the carts must be guarded, otherwise, Tispaquin would attack the carts and take the provisions. So, when Church gets close to the town, he and two other riders ride into town to bring guards out to the carts so they could be free to follow after Tispaquin. He was also told that Bradford was in the Tavern and wanted to speak with him, but he begged off of that as well. They do so and are freed from the mundane duty and go to chase down Tispaquin. So, they chased Tispaquin towards Assawompsett. They crossed Long Pond River which connects Long pond and Assawompsett and into the small neck of land between the two bodies of water, whereupon they were fired at by the Indians. The hunter had become the hunted. They rode a little deeper into the neck and rested the horses in a good valley. After this they got out of that land about ten miles, found a fairly safe place in a thicket to rest and get some sleep. He set up six different guards to work in pairs on two hour shifts so that the whole crew could get some rest. But the men had hardly gotten any sleep in the last 48 hours or more and everyone, including the guards fell sound asleep. Church wakes up, realizing that he had slept for four hours, as did everyone else. He rouses the whole company, gets over to the lookout area viewing the Acushnet River and he sees Indians following their tracks. Again, the hunter is being hunted. So, Church regroups his men, and they start to follow the trackers tracks, or at least, someone's tracks. They soon come upon Little Eyes and his family. Little Eyes is the Sakonnet who threaten to kill Church at the meeting with Awashonks at Treaty Rock. He left the tribe when they made peace with the English. The Indians asked Church if he now wanted to kill Little Eyes. Church tells him "It was not the Englishman's fashion to seek revenge; and that he should have the same quarter, the rest had."[15] But he did capture him put he and his family on a small island in the Acushnet River with his cousin Lightfoot as a guard in case any English came by and tried to kill him. The English knew Lightfoot. They spent another night out in these parts in an apple orchard which the Indians obviously came through. They had taken the apples already. They lit no fires that night because they were being hunted as well. Fortunately for them it was the height of summer. In the morning Church and crew were able to find out where the Indians had slept the night before. They followed the tracks until they came to the Country Road where there was a fork. One set of tracks went one way, and another went in the other direction. Here Church decides to split the company up into two parts. He wanted the Indians to choose which way to go, and the English the other and then to meet at the ruins of John Cooks House in Acushnet. The Indians were not so sure of this idea. Church was but, because he wanted to prove their trustworthiness; of which he was sure, but few other Englishmen were, he put them to the test. The Sakonnets were as brave as any other warriors, but what if they ran into other Englishmen, not as trusting of the Indians as Church? But he insisted. Well, to make a long story short Churches group came upon a group of Indian women picking what Church called Hurtleberries, blueberries."

"They fought the Blueberry Battle?" Toby asks. All the boys breakout in laughter.

---

[15] Ibid 110

"He fought a bunch of women" one boy says.

"Next they come to the women cleaning clothes at the river," says another.

"The Blueberry Battle," the boys all said.

"Captain Church and the Great Blueberry Battle," the boys could not get enough of it.

Temple, slightly aggravated, lets the foolishness go on for a while.

"Well, you know if you put some powder in your musket and add some blueberries in there and fire it off and you get a real good pie," says Temple.

"Yeah, you first," yells out Smith.

"Okay, Okay, settle down now," said Temple. "The Great Blueberry Battle, I'll have to remember that. But there's more to come."

"What's next? The Pumpkin Toss Fight? The Cranberry Conflict?" Smith yells out.

"The Mellon Massacre," someone yells from the back of the room.

"The Apple Orchard Attack," says another.

Everyone laughed themselves silly as each man or boy tries to top the other with fruited exploits.

Temple just stands there with his arms crossed, letting everybody get their laughs in. He has momentarily lost control of his audience, so he waits for them to come back and want more of the story. After a few more minutes of dumb jokes and uproarious laughter Temple finally asks:

"So, are you ready for the next part, or do we call it quits for the night!" Demands Temple.

"No, no, we want more Captain Church. We won't make fun of him again," says Toby.

"Okay, I'm sure he'd like a good laugh too some time," says Temple.

"Anyhow, I'll get you later Smith," Temple says as Smith shakes his hands in a false example of fear. But Temple has the room again.

"So, Church takes the captives, as do the Indians, they got the same amount of people and they return to Plymouth," said Temple. "What Church doesn't know at the time is that it was Philip himself who had been trying to hunt down Church. The hunter truly became the hunted for a while. Philip had waited for Church and his company to return through Assawompset Neck, but it was not Church's habit to go back the way that he came into a country."

"Now over the weeks, Church was able to capture many of the former enemy," Temple recounted. "Some of it was because many had given up the fight, some knew that they could get good terms off of Church, but part of it was that the English army did aid Church in his endeavors. Bradford may have lacked the ingenuity and the daring that Church exemplified, but he did put a lock on the Plymouth Colony. Philip had made a grave mistake by going south, to his home territory. His movement was limited. He no longer could seek aid from the Narragansetts. He could not go to Connecticut. The English, Pequots and Mohegans would eat him up. He had been violently chased out of the west and New York by the Mohawks. To the north the Nipmucks had given up the fight. The Penacook of the Merrimack River area at the base of Maine and New Hampshire had never wanted anything to do with the war from its start, and had renewed a friendship agreement with the English. So, by going to Plymouth Philip was a dangerous and cornered animal. Still, Church was curious as to why the Indians had done so well against the English at the beginning. He asked some of his warriors and they gave him two reasons."

> 'The Indians always took care in their Marches and Fights, not to come too thick together. But the English always kept in a heap together, that it was as easy to hit them as it was to hit a House. The other was, that if at any time they discovered a company of English soldiers in the Woods, they knew that there was all, for the English never scattered; but the Indians always divided and scattered.'[16]

"You can add a few more things to that list," said Temple. "The Indians disguised themselves with tree branches and leaves and blended

---

[16] Ibid 123

right into the forest. The English were not as bright and garish as say, the British red coat uniforms were, but they did not try in any way to blend into the forest. The English saw the forest as something dark and evil, that needed to be cut down, cultivated, and made to be pristine plots of land to be sold to the next influx of Englishmen. To the Indian, it was his home, his hunting grounds, and a welcoming place. The English wanted a pitched battle on a flat piece of land where both sides would line-up and fire away at each other. The Indians never gave them that pleasure. The English thought that it was unmanly and barbaric to fight in the way that the Indians did, but for the longest time, the Indians were winning most of the war. And finally, the fatal flaw of most successful victors: resting on your laurels. After the English's easy victory in the Pequot war of 1637, the English thought that they would be able to subdue the Indians fairly quickly if their worst fears happened and they were at war with the Indians. And they fought the King Philips War in 1675 with the same guns they had used in 1637 even though the technology had improved and the flintlocks outperformed the matchlock. The Indians started the war with the new flintlocks that they had recently bought. The English went to war with yesterday's matchlocks. There were many reasons for the poor start that the English had at the beginning of the war. Very slowly they learned. The English's numeric superiority in population, better access to modern technology, the musket and gunpowder, and finally realizing that they needed help from the Praying Indians, helped to turn the tide for English. And just as the Magistrates welcomed Benjamin Church back into the fold and the governor accepted his deal with Awashonks, and even the Indian hating Moseley grudgingly recognized he needed Indian scouts, the English changed their attitudes, some of them anyhow. There were many lessons to be learned from the Indians. The Sakonnets insisted upon silence when pursuing the enemy. No talking was allowed. The English would give themselves away often by chattering. Creaking leather shoes had to go, even the swishing of a thick pair of pants could alert an enemy. If communication was necessary, they would use a constantly changing vocabulary of animal calls and sounds. A wolf's howl, bird chirpings, and the like. The most important thing, and one that might have saved Churches life near Assawompset Pond, never leave a swamp the same way that you came into it. There would be an ambush waiting there to kill you and your men. These were words that Church could, and did live by. But the war isn't over yet. It will not be until Philip is brought to heel, and that has not happened yet."

"Sunday July 30, 1676 Church was relaxing in the Sunday Church Service in the Plymouth Meeting hall," said Temple. "Governor Winslow himself comes in and gets him out of the service and tells him that there is Indian activity in the Bridgewater area, and he asks Church to round up his troops and get out as fast as he can. He went to the Plymouth Storehouse to get provisions for his troops, but there was no bread for him. So, he had to go house to house, begging bread for the excursion and did so in time to get his troops underway "by the beginning of the afternoon exercise." He left with 40 men, half Indian, half of them English. By the time that he got to the outskirts of Bridgewater it was late at night, so they decided to make camp and move at dawn. They heard some gunplay in the distance, but not enough to make them dare a night excursion, so they stayed where they until dawn. As it was the townsfolk had risen-up and defeated the Indians, capturing 17 of them. It was no loss to Church; they were all on the same side. The main prize, Philip, was in the area and still on the loose."

"Soon Church would spot Philip," said Temple. "They were tracking the Indians through the woods and came upon a tree that had been felled across a river, it was the same spot that the night before the Bridgewater men had fought the Indians. Now there was a lone Indian sitting on the far end of the stump. Church raised his rifle to shoot, but was prevented when one of his Indians told him to stop, he was a friend. The man with Church yells out to the other Indian, who upon looking up, all recognized him as Philip. He jumped off of the log and ran as fast as he could into the woods. Church again tried to get a shot off but missed the moving target. He then crossed the log bridge and tried to run after Philip, but the fleet rabbit had had too much of a head start, and Church could not find him. But they were tantalizingly close. Church never blames the Indian who shouted out to Philip mistakenly in his book, but instead carries on. They still had a very valuable prize.

The Indians were traveling with their families in tow. Just as Philip's troops had nowhere to go, neither did their women and children. And as Philip and his men fought and hid and raced around Plymouth, the women, not being as fast, being burdened with the young, the babies and the old and infirmed where constantly being scooped up by the English and they became prisoners. Often, these women became a great source of intelligence for the English as to who it was that the English were chasing, or how many warriors they had with them. Plus, this time Church and his men had captured Philip's wife Wootonekanuska, and their nine-year-old son. Church and his men get the information that the group includes Narragansetts as well as the Wampanoags, and Philip and resume the tracking and chasing. They came again to a river crossing, possibly the Taunton River again, because it meanders and winds its way from Bridgewater to the Sakonnet River and Mount Hope Bay meandering its way through many Plymouth towns. After wading through the Taunton River, Church gives up the chase momentarily, realizing he had to take care of other responsibilities, including the prisoners at Bridgewater. But the Indians under his command wanted to continue the chase, and he granted them permission, making Light-foot their chief and Captain. On the next day, the Indians came to Church with thirteen more prisoners, and again new information that they were right on the heels of Philip and his men. Apparently, according to these prisoners he still had many warriors who were with him. You might find it curious that these prisoners were giving up so much information, but as we saw with Sagamore John, some of them had given up hope of winning this war, and just wanted it to end. Also, the Indians fighting alongside of Church were often from the same tribe, or even relatives of the Indians. So, it isn't all that surprising that they were giving the English such good information. And Church was offering easy terms for them to surrender themselves, much better than they could have expected from someone like Moseley or even Major Talcott of the Connecticut forces. Moseley was a brute and a hater of the Indians, but Talcott would also slaughter men women and children with hardly a thought of it. He would allow the Indians to have prisoners of other tribes that they could torture. One way was by cutting off the fingers and toes of a captive, one by one until he bleeds to death. Talcott would refer to this as heathenistic barbarity, all the while watching it take place. So, Church showed a better English face to the defeated Indians. He also reminded them that if they didn't comply, he would chase them down and kill them, but that didn't seem to be needful. In fact, Church's men were never numerous and at one point he had to tell his prisoners that he could not spare men to guard them, but that they were to wait until the firing of a coming battle was over and that they must follow his tracks and come to him. He knew that they had the capacity to do so."

"An Indian is next to a bloodhound to follow a track,"[17] Temple said, quoting Church.

"Still, Philip's mindset is on the offense," said Temple. "At one-point Church sent out two soldiers to track where Philip was, and they came upon two Indians tracking down Church's whereabouts. The Indians screamed and yelled as an alarm for Philip and crew to run away, and they did, leaving their breakfast food cooking on the skillet and spit as they fled capture. They ran into a small swamp which Church and his men surrounded, sending Isaac Howland on one side, and himself on the other. They both converged on the other end of the swamp just as the Indians were coming out, surprised to see the English and Indians in a large force waiting for them. Church in his book claims that he commanded the Indians telling them:

> "If they fired one gun they were all dead men; for he would have them know(that) he had them hemmed in with a force sufficient to command them; but if they peaceably surrender'd they should have good quarter."[18]

"They gave up without firing a shot," said Temple. "Philip was not among them, nor his top Captains. They waited in the Swamp to watch the fight, that didn't take place, and then doubled back on their track, like a fox trying to throw a dog off a trail. Church then ventured into the

---

[17] Ibid 132
[18] Ibid 133

swamp, found some of Philips men fought a battle with them, killing some. Thomas Lucas of Plymouth was shot and killed by the Indians as they exited the swamp. Church and two of his men were chasing three Indians, two of which surrendered, Church ran after the third. He had long hair that was tied on the top of his head with a rattlesnake skin which hung down part of his back as he ran. Church assumed that it was Totoson, the chieftain who led the raid on Clark's garrison in Plymouth. It was not he, but another Indian. Church pursuing him, got within good shooting distance, put his rifle up and fired, but the charge misfired. Somehow the Indian heard the misfire, turned, raising his weapon which also misfired. The dampness of the morning made both their powder wet. So, the Indian turned to run again, got tripped up by a vine and fell face first into the ground. Church rammed his musket into the back of his head, killing him instantly. As Church is catching his breath looking over the dead man another one "come flying at him like a dragon"[19] and they start fighting hand to hand. Other English soldiers had been chasing this "dragon" and shot at him while Church and he were struggling. Church claims to have felt the wind of the bullets whizzing past him, but he was unharmed, the "dragon" Indian fell dead."

"When they assessed the day's action, they figured that they had killed and captured 173 people," said Temple. "They were out of food, so they set off to Bridgewater, including those prisoners who they had told to wait on them until the fighting was over. Church claims that his men celebrated their victory, but also the captured Indians did as well."

> 'The prisoners laughed as loud as the soldiers, not being so (well) treated for a long time… Some of the Indians said to Capt. Church 'Sir, you have made Philip ready to dye, for you have made him as poor, and miserable as he used to make the English.'[20]

---

[19] Ibid 136
[20] Ibid 138

"The next day, Friday August 4th, 1676, Church arrived at Plymouth with his men and the prisoners," said Temple. "They rested up for a couple of days before Church headed out again, this time to Dartmouth. They were looking for Totoson, the one who lead the attack on Clark's garrison house. They did not find him, he had escaped, but they found his father, Sam Barrow, who was also known to be involved in the Clark house burning. His Indian name was Sanballett. When Church encountered him, Church told the old man that he had orders to not show leniency to Sanballett, that he was to be executed. As a warrior, he understood this, but requested that he be able to smoke some tobacco one last time. Church wrote about Sanballette's reaction:

> 'The sentence of death against him was just, and that he was indeed ashamed to live any longer, and desired no more favor than to Smoke a Whiff of Tobacco before his execution.'[21]

"After a couple of whiffs, Sanballett said that he was ready and one of Church's Indians sunk his hatchet into the old warrior's head," Temple said.

"Totoson had escaped with his eight-year-old son and an old squaw to Agawam, in Wareham," said Temple. "They all must have been ill before this episode because first the son died mysteriously, then Totoson, and the squaw survived long enough make it to Sandwich, tell the story of their deaths, offer to show people where she buried them, then got sick herself and died. So Totoson was gone. Philip had very few of his Captains and advisors left, but the real question was, how many warriors did he still have with him and more importantly, were they still loyal?"

"Church returns to Plymouth, looking for some rest, got none, but was sent out this time to Pocasset," said Temple. "He was there for a while, but did not see any hostile Indians. So, he got on the Ferry with about a half dozen of his men taking him to Aquidneck Island to go see his wife at Mr. Sanford's house. She was so surprised to see him that she fainted when he appeared. Unfortunately for her, once she revived,

---

[21] Ibid 140

horsemen were riding in to speak to Captain Church. They were Major Sanford and Captain Roger Golding (the captain who saved Church and his men at the Pease Field Fight)."

"They asked him, 'What he would give to hear some News of Philip?' He replied, 'That was what he wanted.'"[22]

"They told Church that they had an Indian who had just fled from Philip," said Temple. "He claimed that Philip had killed his brother for suggesting that he make peace with the English. That was the last thing that Philip wanted to hear, so he killed the man. After that, his brother escaped and now wanted revenge for his brother and would show the English where he was. He was in Mount Hope, just a ferry ride across the Mount Hope Bay. Church and company saddled up to ride again. Actually, their mounts had never been unsaddled. So, they rode off before they lost the sunlight. It is the evening of Friday August 11th, 1676. His poor wife probably fainted again."

"The two men rode with Church and joined him in the hunt for Philip," said Temple. "According to the informant's information, Philip's camp was in a high ground near a swamp. In case of an attack, he could escape into the swamp and either hide, or make his further escape. Church decided to set an ambush. Captain Golding was offered the post of watching and attacking "beating up" Philip's headquarters. He would be the spring to of the trap, the ambush. It was to set into motion at daybreak."

> "He told him also that his custom was to creep with his company on their bellies, until they came as near as they could; and as soon as the enemy discovered them they would cry out; and that was the word to fire and fall on."[23]

"Golding was to shout and make as much noise as he could as he chased Philip once he was flushed out of his liar," said Temple. "The Indians fleeing would have no need to be yelling; Goulding and his

---

[22] Ibid 128
[23] Ibid 145

men would be. Church assumed that Philip would be the first to run towards the swamp. "'Capt. Church knowing that it was Philips custom to be fore-most in the flight.'"[24]

"The rest of the men would set themselves up in front of the swamp in order to stop, or kill Philip," said Temple. "It was early August, so first light would come early, around 4:30 am. They just had to lay in wait. Before Church could get completely set, a gun had fired. He thought that it was an accident, but the trap had already been sprung. One of the Indians had gone outside of the camp to relieve himself and Golding or one of his men thought that they had been discovered, rose up and shot. The battle was on. Most of Golding's men shot high because the Indians were not even out of their bedding. But the Indians, once startled, were racing towards the swamp. Philip only had on his "small breeches and stockings" threw his "Petunk," satchel, and powder horn over his head, grabbed his gun and then ran as fast as he could toward the swamp. He was also running straight at two of Churches men hiding in the ambush, one an Englishman, the other an Indian. The Englishman took the first shot, it misfired. He told the Indian to shoot, he did and hit his target. They were able to get off two shots, two inches above the heart, the other directly through it. Philip, the King of the Wampanoags was dead, face down in the muddy water of an early August morning. Another Indian yelled out 'Iootash, Iootash, (fight, fight,)' so the battle continued. Church asked his Indian aid, Peter, 'Who that was that yelled for them to continue fighting,' and Peter said that it was Philip's chief Captain, Annowan. The men who shot Philip came and bragged about their deed; Church told them to be silent about it until they had cleared the swamp. As it was, the remainder of the Indians had fled, but Philip, the enemy of all enemies was dead."

"With that boys, we will call it a night," said Temple.

"Wow!... they got him," exclaimed Toby. "But what about Annawon?? "Is that all? What do they do with Philips body? Is the war over?"

"So many questions, but it is late. We will wrap it all up tomorrow," said Temple.

---

[24] Ibid 145

CHAPTER ELEVEN

Annawon

Annawon's rock, Rehoboth Massachusetts. TUSOE.org

"Mr. Temple, Mr. Temple," Toby and Jeremiah yell as they came running up to the storyteller as he walks up to the door of the barracks for this night's story of the King Philips War.

"How come the war didn't end with Philip's death. Wasn't it all about him? What did they do with the body?" the young boys blurt out.

"That's what I'll talk about tonight," said Temple. "Time to go in now."

"Okay, will do," Toby says as he squeezes past Temple and the door jam.

"No manners," Jeremiah says as he shakes his head at his impetuous friend. Then runs over to join Toby as the other boys race in saying "excuse me, pardon me, excuse me," as they greet Mr. Temple.

Timmy is the last boy to approach the door and he dared not squeeze by Temple.

"Go on in young man," Temple says pointing with his open hand as he steps away from the door to make room. The boy gladly does so saying, "Thank you sir," as he runs in.

Temple walks in, smiling. The small hut is packed with boys and men and a couple of the wives, including Bridget. He loved telling the story of Captain Church, and tonight would be the last part. Before he starts, he rearranges the room.

"Toby, you were rude when you came in the door. You squeezed right past me to rush in to get the best spot. I want you to give up your spot to Timmy, in the back," said Temple.

"But that's not fair, I was here first," said Toby.

"Just my point," said Temple. "The Bible says that 'the last shall be first, and the first shall be last.' Didn't your mother ever teach you about manners?"

"My Mom died," Toby murmurs.

"So sorry about that, but your Father remarried, right?" Temple queried.

"Yes sir," Toby says.

"What did she teach you?" Temple asks.

"To mind your elders," Toby meekly replied.

"Then you ought to of listened to her," Bridget speaks out.

"Yes Mam," Toby says completely mortified as he heads to the back of the hut.

Smith pulls Toby by his side rubbing his head, as Timmy clambers over the other boys to get to the front next to Jeremiah.

Temple smiles at Bridget, and says, "Okay boys take your seats and we'll get on with it. Remember, the things that you learn here at this fort will help us win the war and hopefully save your lives, so that you can live free."

Temple was happy and sad, because he had enjoyed every minute of the storytelling, even the out-of-control moments. But he knew that this story was helping to build the minds, not only of the boys, but the men who heard it and shared it. Some of the officers had already been asking him to repeat the story to others. There was not a spare foot in the 12-foot by 14-foot hut, but no one complained. Temple proceeds to his spot near the fireplace as he begins to speak.

"So last night we talked about the killing of Philip," Temple said. "Some of you might think that the war is over with his death. Not so fast. There is still his second in command, Annawon, who must be dealt with, and even after that there will be some mop-up activity."

"Mop-up, oh boy, when does it all end," Toby says incredibly.

"When Church goes home, and even then, he gets recalled by the Governor on occasions when there are some renegade Indians to be arrested," said Temple. "But we are getting ahead of ourselves. Philip has been killed. Church gathers all the men together and tells them and they all gave three loud Huzzas."

"Hip hip Hooray, hip hip hooray, hip hip hooray," the boys stood up and shouted.

"Yeah, kind of like that," said Temple. "They go to the body and drag it out of the puddle Philip fell into in his death fall, to a dry spot. They grabbed him by his stockings and his small breeches, which was all he had on. The body was a 'doleful, great, naked, dirty beast,' Church claimed. Then he added:

> "That foreasmuch as he caused many an Englishman's body to lye unburied and rot above ground, that not one of his bones should be buried."[25]

"He then called an Indian executioner to behead the body and cut him in quarters," Temple reported. "It was the normal thing to do to a

---

[25] Ibid 150

person's body when they had rebelled against the king. As the English saw it, he had rebelled against the English rule there in Plymouth which was a representation of the king, hence, he had rebelled against the king and received a rebel's sentence. The man who was to cut him up made a short speech over him."

> "Philip, he had been a very great man, and had made many a man afraid of him, but so big as he was he would now chop his ass for him."[26]

"With that, the Indian went to work cutting him up," Temple said. "Captain Church gave the head and one of his hands to Alderman, the Indian who shot him. Philip's head would ultimately wind up on a pole in Plymouth visible for all to see, the hands went to Boston. But Alderman made money showing off his war trophies in the meantime. Afterwards, Church and company relaxed in Portsmouth for a couple of days, then on the 15th of August they crossed the Sakonnet River and ranged through the woods until they came to Plymouth on the 17th. While they were there, a letter came to the governor claiming that Annawon was in the Swansea/Rehoboth area, causing havoc there. Having just been paid, Church complained about the rate of pay, claiming that he wasn't sure if anyone would muster-up again, but they did. He got Jabez Howland, his Lieutenant and others and they got Captain Lightfoot and his Indian crew. So, they were off on the hunt again, but found nothing in Pocasset. They went to Aquidneck Island for a little rest when on a Sunday morning, a letter came claiming that a number of Indians had been seen canoeing from Prudence Island in Narraganset Bay to Papasquash Neck on the west side of the Mount Hope peninsula. It is almost an island, but is connected by a small sliver of land to the west side of Mount Hope. Church and his Indians canoe over there, but as they do so, the wind is picking up. By the Time Howland is ready to go over with the English part of his company, the water is too rough for traveling by canoe. So Church is on Mount Hope with just his Indians about 16 of them. The

---

[26] Ibid 151

English would rejoin them the next day. In the meanwhile, Church and his Indian crew made some good headway. They captured ten warriors along with their wives and children. A recent captive turned soldier for Church helped to bring these men in and convince them to surrender. One of them wanted to go and retrieve his father and a squaw who were a few miles away in Rehoboth. Church would go with him, bringing a few men, hoping to get some good information about Annawon. All he knew right now was that Annawon never "roosted" in one place for long. So, he went a couple miles northeast to Rehoboth, where Annawon had originally been sighted. The small crew, one Englishman, who had met up with Church's band, and a few Indians make their way to a swamp in Rehoboth. The new Indian soldier gives out a wolf howl to communicate with his father. He does so again and soon he got a howl in reply. Church allows him to go get his father. While they are waiting for their return, Church spots a human track of some sort in the ground and examines it. They can hear people returning. They hide in the bushes. Soon, an old man with a rifle resting on his shoulder, a young woman and the new soldier return. The men jump up, surrounding the two new captives, and hold them securely. Church interrogates them both and it turns out they have both recently seen Annawon. The old man agrees to lead them to the Indian chief, he is honor bound because Church did not take his life when by all rights, he could have. But there is a problem. Annawon has 50 to 60 warriors with him. Church has six. He talks to the men to see if they are up to the task at hand. If they wait until morning or until they get more men, Annawon may escape. The Indians told him:

> 'They were always ready to obey his commands, &c. But withal told him, That they knew this Captain Annawon was a great soldier; that he had been a valiant Captain under Asuhmequn, Philip's father, and that he had been Philip's chieftain all this war; a very subtle man, and of great resolution, and had often said, that he would never be taken alive by the English… that it would be a pity

that after all the great things that he (Church) had done, he should throw away his life at last.'²⁷

Church claimed that they were right in all they said, but then stated:

"If they would cheerfully go with him, the same Almighty Providence that had hitherto protected and befriended them would do so still."²⁸

"The Indians said that they would go," said Temple. "Then he turned to the one Englishman with him, Cook, and asked him what he thought. He replied: 'I am never afraid of going anywhere when you are with me.'²⁹

"The mission was on, there was little daylight left and they would have to follow the old man and the young squaw to Annawon," said Temple. "The old man said that he would lead Church to Annawon, but he would not fight his old friend and ally, but he would protect Church."

"The old man was fleet of foot as he outpaced everyone in Church's Band," said Temple. "Then he sits down. The group catches up to him. Church asks him, 'What News?' He states that Annawon usually sends out guards right at dusk and they return before the sun has set. So, he is giving them time to run their course. Not far off they can hear a sound. Church motions for everyone to be silent. Momentarily he asks, what do you think it is. They concluded that it was the sound of someone pounding something with a mortar. To be able to hear that, they had to be very close. They were near their camp. It was behind a large rock wall. On the side that Church and company were, it was a steep rounded top rock about 15 to 20 feet high. They crawl up it to the edge. On the other side it was a sheer drop of about 30 feet. There are some footholds and handholds on the face of it that you could climb down by. At the base was a large clearing with four fires going. Three were for Annawon's men. The fourth, at the base of the rock was where

---

²⁷ Ibid 164
²⁸ Ibid 164
²⁹ Ibid 165

Annawon and his son lay. There was a felled tree with birch branches lined up against it. There nearby a roaring fire with Annawon's dinner was cooking. Their arms were all together in one place leaning against a stick that rested in the crotch of two trees. There was a covering over them to protect them from any dampness from dew or rain. Annawon's feet, and his son's head were right next to the guns. Church sent the old man and the squaw down first to divert attention from the rest of the crew. Church followed the old man grasping a hatchet in his hand. This was the only way of getting in without being shot. And nobody really paid any heed to the intruders as they descended the rock wall. When he gets down, he is spotted by the son who hides himself in his blanket. Church secures the guns, Annawon spots him, shouts out 'Howoh' 'Who is that?' Instantly he realizes that he can't escape, but neither does he fight. According to Church's book, he states Annawon "threw himself back again, and lay silently until Captain Church secured all the arms."[30] Then he sent his men out to the fires in the camp. They told the Indians that they were surrounded. That it was in their best interest to submit peacefully or else Captain Church would cut them all down. Church's men being Indians, except for Cook, could speak to them in their language, and told them if they turned in their guns and stayed peaceful, that it would go well for them. They complied. They turned in all their weapons, their guns, their hatchets. Church's men gathered them, brought them to Church. So, the great Annawon had been captured, without a shot being fired."

"Why didn't they fight?" Asked Toby.

"Sometimes you just loose the will to fight," said Temple. "When you know that your cause is hopeless. You are tired of the fight, of running, losing your home, your women, always hungry, always cold, never really able to sleep because every little noise sounds like someone sneaking up on you. And besides, they had seen their leader get killed as he was running away from a fight. And for all they knew, Church did have an army surrounding them. Bradford's army was never that far away. They must have had it. They had run out of strength and will power."

---

[30] Ibid 168

"With that, Church asked Annawon what he had for dinner," said Temple. "Church told him that he was come to 'sup with you,' which was actually an accepted expectation of a guest from an Indian host, though this was most unexpected. Annawon asked him if he wanted horse beef or cow beef. Church said the cow beef. He pulled the salt packet that he always carried in his pocket and salted it, then added some dried green corn, (which was what was being ground in the mortar that they had heard earlier) and it made for a hearty supper. When the supper was ended, he sent his men to speak again to Annawon's men. They reminded all there that Church's men were the ones who had killed Philip, that all the Indian armies were now subdued, basically stating that the war was over. They told Annawon's men that they had also captured the other ten warriors who went to Mount Hope, along with all the women and children. Church's men instructed the captives that they should remain where they were until morning when they would march to Tiverton where the Indians would be reunited with their friends and family. Those who complied with Churches wishes would be treated well."

Annawon's men complied.

"Church now tried to take a nap, but sleep never came to him," Temple reported. "He looked on his men, all of them, and the Indians were fast asleep. He looked at Annawon, he was wide awake as well. They just stared at each other for about an hour. He never said anything to him because he could not speak the Wampanoag language, and he thought that Annawon couldn't speak English. (Annawon had asked Church if he wanted horse-flesh or cow-flesh, but knowing rudimentary terms is not the same as speaking the language.) Then Annawon got up and walked off some distance. Church thought that he was going to relieve himself, but he remains gone for some time. Church was getting nervous. Church got close to the guns and Annawon's son. If Annawon comes in with a gun, he would risk shooting his son. Then Church hears someone approaching from the same direction that Annawon had walked. By the light of the moon, church could see that it was Annawon, and that he was carrying something. He walks over to Church, kneels before him and presents him with gifts. He spoke in plain English:

'Great Captain, you have killed Philip, and conquered his country for I believe, that I and my company are the last that war against the English, so suppose that the war is ended by your means; and therefore these things belong to you.'[31]

"It was Philip's wampum belts, nine inches wide made out of polished sea shells," said Temple. "It was Philip's status symbol and used as money by Indians and Englishmen alike. When it was hung on Church around his shoulders, it reached down to his ankles. It had pictures and symbols on it of birds and animals. It was very ornate. There was also one for his head. He pulled out two horns of glazed powder, and a red cloth blanket. These were "Philip's Royalties" Annawon said. Then Annawon and Church spent the night talking about what mighty successes that he had had for Asuhmequin, (Philip's father Massasoit)."

"In the morning they all marched down the road towards Taunton," said Temple. "They met-up with the rest of the crew and the other captives. They spent a day there and were very well received by the town. From there he goes to Aquidneck Island, with Annawon and six of his warriors, as he has his Lieutenant bring the rest of the captives and the crew to Plymouth. He stays on the island a couple of days before heading to Plymouth with everyone including Alice and his two boys. Finally, they were going home, to Duxbury. Church is treated like a hero as the people welcomed he and his wife back to town. Alice's parents, the Southworth's were more than happy to see their daughter and family back again."

"That's my son and grandsons there," Magistrate Southworth beams, elevating his son-in-law to actual son. He shakes hands with all the people glowing in Church's popularity like a gladhanding politician," said Temple.

"The festivities are short-lived as in a couple of days, Church's services were needed again," reports Temple. "He headed out and was able to convince another of Philip's Captains Tispaquin to give himself

---

[31] Ibid 172

up, his wife and child were already being held captive in Plymouth, so he surrendered. Church stops in Boston, Governor John Leverett, who was on his deathbed wanted to see the hero himself. The prisoner was sent ahead of him. Leverett promised Church a pension for his efforts, but since he died soon thereafter, nothing ever came of it. When Church came to Plymouth, he was grieved to see that the heads of Annawon and Tispaquin were on poles outside of the town. He never promised them that they would be pardoned, but he had hoped for it."

"But why did he care for them?" asked Toby. "They were the enemies."

"Yes, they were, but sometimes, if the roles were reversed, if Church were an Indian and Annawon an Englishman…" Temple wonders outloud.

"You're daft" says Smith. "Church was as much an Indian as I am."

"Maybe," said Temple. "But he learned from them. Maybe he saw them as fellow soldiers. Or maybe he thought of himself as a fellow warrior. But he took no pleasure in seeing their heads hoisted on a pole."

"But the war, the war is over," Temple continues in a calm tone. "There were more fights in Maine and elsewhere, but in the three United Colonies, and Rhode Island, there is peace. It had been a costly war in lives in farmland, and it scarred the landscape. The Wampanoags as a tribe were wiped out. Some English towns wouldn't rebuild for a decade. It was devasting, but it was over. The people could celebrate that."

"Hip, hip, hooray, for Captain Church, hip, hip hooray, for Captain Church," the boys all shout, as they pick-up their drums and march out of the barracks, making a huge fuss and parading around the grounds, keeping others awake, wondering what was going on.

The boys kept drumming and shouting "Captain Church won the war! Captain Church won the war! Captain Church won the war!" pounding away on their drums.

www.ingramcontent.com/pod-product-compliance
Lightning Source LLC
Chambersburg PA
CBHW021447070526
44577CB00002B/288